The Creative Art of Sewing

Joan Fisher

HAMLYN
London · New York · Sydney · Toronto

The author gratefully acknowledges the help
given with the preparation of this book
by Simplicity Patterns Limited.

Published by
The Hamlyn Publishing Group Ltd
London · New York · Sydney · Toronto
Hamlyn House, Feltham, Middlesex, England

ISBN 0 600 31758 7

Printed in Holland by Henkes Senefelder bv, Purmerend
Bound by Proost & Brandt Bookbinders, Amsterdam

Contents

Introduction

Dressmaking must surely be one of the most rewarding forms of handicraft. There is great pleasure to be found in simply choosing with care the raw materials—harmonising colour, texture and style—then going on to create a beautiful finished product. Added to this is the satisfaction of being able to wear your 'work of art' . . . Sewing your own clothes is also a moneysaving proposition, for perfectly-fitted garments tailor-made in every respect to suit you exactly, can be produced for a fraction of the cost of ready-made clothes. It is thus easier and cheaper to keep up with constantly changing fashion trends.

Once a particular basic style is fitted to your shape and size, it can be used over and over again, made up in totally different fabric types and designs to create a wardrobe of fashionable clothes. The same classic shift, for instance, will look totally different made up in a rich jewel-bright velvet as it will in a polka-dotted cotton print, and different again in a supple, stretchy knit fabric. Add further contrast with a careful choice of accessories, belts and jewellery—and no one would ever guess all the dresses came from the same original pattern. In fact, part of the real and final satisfaction in sewing your own clothes is that friends never do guess your outfit is home-made!

Almost anyone can sew pieces of fabric together to make a dress. But it takes a good deal more skill, imagination and application to give this basic dress a couture finish. In this book I aim to show you how easy it is to learn the art of sewing, for it is indeed an art: the art of finishing your garments so they fit perfectly, reflect your personality and way of life, and never—in any circumstances—look 'home-made'.

JOAN FISHER

Back to basics

TOOLS AND EQUIPMENT

As with any other craft, if you intend to take your sewing seriously, and to produce neat, professional-looking work, it is essential you have all the necessary tools of the trade. Never try to make do with inadequate or poor-quality equipment, accessories or gadgets—it just is not worth it. Scissors which are not as sharp as they should be, needles which are the wrong size for the job, thread which is unsuitable for a particular fabric . . . small details perhaps, but they are enough to spoil your finished garment, and an insult to the time and effort you might have spent in the sewing.

Ideally a room should be set aside for your sewing activities—if this is not possible, then a corner of a room will do, somewhere where you can have your machine permanently in position, in a good light and with a chair at a comfortable height for working. Your equipment, tools and gadgets should be kept conveniently to hand, and in neat order. Bookshelves on the wall nearby can take your sewing books, leaflets and patterns. A felt noticeboard or section of cork on the wall is also useful for pinning up design ideas, pattern envelopes, cuttings from papers or magazines.

The following list represents the ideal collection of equipment the home dressmaker should possess. Some items however do fall into the luxury class, and it is perfectly possible to produce attractive work without owning these items—it should be fairly obvious which these luxury items are. Also, the tools you collect naturally should bear some relation to the type of sewing you intend to do—if you are unlikely, for instance, ever to make up garments in velvet or any other pile fabric, then a velvet board will be unnecessary.

Needles. Have a good supply of different sizes of both machine and hand-sewing needles. For hand-sewing, No. 7 darners are best for basting, and No. 9 sharps or straws for fine work. 'Sharps' are all-purpose, round-eyed needles of medium length; 'betweens' are short, round-eyed needles used for very fine sewing; 'milliners' are round-eyed, long and slender; they are used for basting, hand-shirring and similar sewing tasks; 'crewels' are medium length with long eyes that make threading easy, and they can carry several strands of thread at the same time. For machine-sewing, use No. 11 for fine fabrics, No. 14 for general use, and No. 16 for heavy fabrics.

Pins. Medium-sized steel ones are best as these will not leave rust marks or holes in your fabric. Pins with brightly-coloured glass heads are also useful, as they are easy to see and handle.

Scissors. Always buy the best-quality scissors and shears, and use them only for fabric, never on paper. As soon as the blades show signs of dullness, have them sharpened. The following list is the ideal selection of types and sizes of scissors and shears for all sewing purposes:

1. Bent-handled shears. These are best for cutting fabric as the blades rest flat on the cutting surface, and you do not have to lift the fabric when cutting round a pattern. Left-handed models are usually available.

2. Trimming scissors. Good for trimming and clipping seams and for general use.

3. Small embroidery scissors. These are useful for cutting buttonholes, threads and other small jobs.

4. Pinking shears. Use these to cut a zigzag edge and for finishing hem edges and seams. Never use pinking shears to cut out a garment.

4. Scalloping shears. These are similar to pinking shears but cut a scalloped edge instead of a zigzag edge. Use them for finishing hem and seam edges too.

Tape measure. A flexible type, made of a material that will not stretch or tear is the wisest choice. The measure should be reversible (markings appear on both sides), have centimetre and inch markings, and have metal tips at each end.

Yardstick. Select a smoothly finished one which will not catch on the fabric. This is used to measure fabric, to check grain lines, and to make your own patterns..

Hem gauge. A measuring device marked with various depths so that hems can be turned and pressed in one step.

Sewing gauge. This is a 6-inch gauge with a moveable indicator. It is convenient for measuring short distances.

Skirt marker. There are two basic types of hem marker available: the type of marker which uses pins is the most accurate, but it does require the help of a second person. The bulb type of marker which uses powdered chalk to mark the hemline on your skirt or dress permits you to do the job on your own.

Stitch unpicker. A useful gadget which will unpick an entire seam in a matter of seconds.

Set square. Essential for drawing right angles and useful for all short straight lines.

Thimble. Even if you think you can manage without one, do persevere—eventually you will find you can work more easily and quickly with it.

Paper. Large sheets of strong white or brown paper for making paper patterns. Small sheets for sketching designs.

A soft pencil. For drawing out paper patterns, sketching your designs, and occasionally for marking wrong side of fabric with guide lines.

Dressmaker's tracing or carbon paper. For transferring pattern markings to fabrics and interfacings. A packet of assorted colours is most convenient, as you can then choose a suitable colour for your fabric—pale-coloured carbon papers are best for light-coloured fabrics, as the darker ones leave too heavy a mark which can sometimes show through on to the right side of the finished garment.

Tracing wheel. Used in conjunction with carbon or tracing paper. The tracing wheel has tiny teeth which are rolled over the carbon paper where the pattern marks are required to be transferred to your fabric. To get a better impression from the carbon and to protect your working surface, slip a piece of heavy cardboard under the fabric before starting to use wheel.

Tailor's chalk. This is used on fabrics which cannot be marked with carbon to transfer pattern markings. Because the chalk rubs off easily, it is used for temporary markings only. Available in different colours, but white and blue are used most often as they are less likely to stain the fabric.

Chalk pencils. Available in colours, and used also to transfer pattern markings to fabric. Because these pencils can be sharpened to a point, they give a thin, accurate line.

Beeswax. Useful for strengthening thread, particularly for sewing on buttons as it also acts as a lubricant. Beeswax can usually be bought in a holder having grooves through which the thread is pulled for waxing.

Basting cotton. Use white for dark-coloured fabrics; pale contrasting colours for light-coloured fabrics. Avoid bright cottons on pale fabrics as traces of colour can sometimes be left behind.

Sewing threads. Again a good varied selection of types, sizes and colours is best. Mercerised cotton is best for most everyday purposes; for heavy fabrics, such as tweed, suiting and corduroy use size 40 mercerised cotton; for lighter weight fabrics, use size 50.

Unmercerised cotton thread is also available in sizes 10–60. No. 40 has the largest shade range.

Button and carpet thread is extra heavy for hand sewing only. Silk thread is strong and has a certain amount of elasticity. It can be used on silk, silk-like and fine wool fabrics. Buttonhole twist is a strong, silk thread with a special twist for making hand-worked buttonholes, sewing on buttons and decorative hand or machine stitching. Synthetic thread is a polyester thread recommended for use on knits, stretch, man-made and most drip-dry fabrics. Its elasticity makes it compatible with knits and other stretch fabrics. There are also excellent multi-purpose threads available which can be used for all sewing purposes, in a wide range of shades.

Iron and ironing board. Careful pressing as you go along is essential for a perfectly finished garment. Keep iron and ironing board conveniently to hand as you work. A combination steam-dry iron is best, with a reliable temperature control for different fabric types. The ironing board should be well-padded.

Sleeve board. A small ironing board for pressing sleeves and difficult-to-reach areas.

Tailor's ham. A firm, rounded cushion for pressing areas that need shaping such as curved darts or seams at shoulder, bust or hip line.

Velvet board. A length of canvas, covered with fine upright wires, which is used for pressing nap and pile fabrics. The pile side of the fabric is pressed over the wire side of the board to prevent it from matting or flattening.

Pressing cloths. These are used to prevent fabrics from getting a shine as sometimes occurs when fabrics come into direct contact with a hot iron. Cheesecloth or muslin pressing cloths are good for cottons and linens; woollen pressing cloths are best for wool fabrics. Use pressing cloths dry over delicate fabrics, damp over linen or cotton.

Pressing mitt. Useful for pressing curves. To make your own

pressing mitt, cut a rectangle of paper 7in. by 9½in. Curve the corners at one end, and use this pattern to cut out three layers of calico. Stitch a ½-in. hem along the straight edge of one layer. Sandwich this layer between other two, and stitch round curved and side edges. Turn right side out, so hemmed edge of first layer is inside mitt. Pad the two unhemmed layers with wool, turn in ½-in. hem on both straight edges and hemstitch neatly together.

Steam dolly. Excellent for quick, efficient pressing of seams. Cut a strip of light-coloured woollen material, 12in. by 2in., and roll up tightly, graduating to a point at one end. Tie a length of tape round centre. To use, the point is dipped in water and drawn along the fold of a seam which is then pressed open with the iron.

Cutting board. If you do not have a large old smooth-surfaced kitchen table or similar flat surface to work on when cutting out patterns, make yourself a cutting board from a piece of hard-board, about 4ft. by 3ft. This can be placed on top of a table, on the floor or even on a bed, and used as a working surface for cutting out and assembling pattern pieces.

Pattern bag. Cut an oblong of strong brown paper, 12in. by 20in. Lay it on a flat surface with shorter edges at top and bottom. Now make a 6-in. fold from lower end, and machine-stitch down sides, to form a 'pocket'. Fold top end down to form a flap, making this fold 8in. from first fold. Keep your patterns in orderly fashion in this bag.

GUIDE TO FABRIC TYPES

Those of you who already make your own clothes will know how exciting fabric shops and departments can be. For new-comers to dressmaking, this is a pleasure still to come! In fact the selection of a suitable fabric can sometimes be difficult because there is such a wonderful range of designs and fabric types from which to choose. Do not however be too bewitched by the attractive eyecatching display—it is important to choose the right weight and design of fabric for the garment you intend to make. It is well worth while spending time in fabric stores and departments just getting to know the many types of fabric available before you actually buy any. Study the labels and discover which fabrics are washable, which are crease-resistant, which need special handling and sewing techniques. The following guide describes a few of the basic fabric types. In general terms, fabrics may be divided into two main groups: woven and knitted. The majority of fabrics are woven.

Cotton. These are plain-weave natural fabrics, firmly woven and available in a wide range of weights and patterns. A light starch when washing cotton garments will help to retain the natural 'crispness' of the fabric.

Batiste. A fine lightweight plain-weave fabric, usually of cotton.

Burlap. A coarse fabric, which is a plain weave of jute, hemp or cotton used for sportswear.

Canvas. Heavy, strong, plain-weave fabric useful for sports-wear. A heavier form of canvas is known as **duck**.

Challis. A soft lightweight worsted cloth available in solid colours or prints. Good for dresses, and for children's wear.

Two simply-styled beach dresses—easy enough for a beginner to make.

Chambray. A cotton fabric with warp threads in a colour, and white used as a filling. The result is an attractive two-tone effect.

Chiffon. A transparent very sheer fabric of highly-twisted silk or synthetic yarns.

Chintz. A glazed plain-weave cotton in solid colours or prints.

Corded fabrics. These are available in different weights, with the cording—or ribbing—in a variety of thicknesses. Corded fabrics include: Bedford cord, broadcloth, poplin and faille.

Crêpe. This refers to the surface texture of a fabric, and can be produced in silk, synthetic, cotton or wool fabrics, from sheer to heavy weights.

Denim. A cotton fabric usually made with coloured warp yarns and lighter or white filling yarns.

Dimity. A sheer crisp cotton which may be plain, checked, striped or printed.

Flannel. Woven of wool, synthetics or blends and generally it has a very lightly napped surface.

Gabardine. A fine, close twill of worsted, cotton or synthetics.

Georgette. Special weave; crinkled fabric, fairly lightweight.

Jacquard weaves. The jacquard loom produces various patterned-weave fabrics. These fabrics include: table linen, brocade (in which gold or silver threads may be used) and damask.

Knitted fabrics. Knit fabrics are made of yarn which is looped together like chain stitches instead of being woven. There are two basic types of fabric: the horizontally knitted fabric which stretches mostly in a crosswise direction, and the vertically knitted fabric which is more tightly woven and with less give than the horizontal knit. Tricot is an example of the vertical knit, with fine vertical ribs on its right side, horizontal on the reverse. Double knits have two layers of fabric, with right and wrong sides almost identical.

Lace. Many varieties available in cotton and silk, ranging from delicate Chantilly lace to sturdy Venise. In some types, the mesh design is outlined in fine embroidery.

Laminated fabrics. Also known as bonded fabrics. These fabrics consist of an outer or face fabric of almost any fibre fused to a lining fabric such as tricot or taffeta. The permanent backing gives stability to the face fabric and prevents stretching.

Lawn. A closely-woven cotton somewhat resembling voile but with more body. May also be made in synthetic fibres.

Linen. Natural fabric which ranges in weight from sheer 'handkerchief' linen to heavy suitings. Occasional thicker places in the yarn give a slightly slubbed effect.

Man-made fabrics or synthetics. This term includes all fabrics made from chemically-produced fibres—rayon, nylon, acetate, Dacron, Orlon, Terylene, Crimplene are just a few of the synthetic fabrics available. All are strong and hardwearing.

Napped fabrics. 'Napping' is a process which lifts the short fibres so they form a hairy or down surface. This nap may be brushed down or left unbrushed. Doeskin, fleece and suede cloth are all napped fabrics.

Organdie. A very lightweight plain-weave cotton with a crisp finish.

Organza. Similar to organdie but of silk or rayon. Used for evening dresses and blouses.

Peau de soie. A satin weave with a lustre duller than satin itself. Comparatively heavy.

Pile fabrics. Pile fabrics are composed of raised loops which are cut so they stand up from the surface. Pile fabrics include velvet, corduroy, fur fabrics, velour and velveteen. It is important when cutting all pile, and also napped. fabrics that the garment pieces are cut with the pile or nap running in the same direction, otherwise the sections of the completed garment will appear to have been cut from different shades of the same colour. Velvet, velveteen and corduroy should all have the pile running towards the top of the garment for the richest and darkest colour.

Pique. A true pique is woven with lengthwise or crosswise ribs; but there are several fabrics commonly referred to as pique which actually are not, as the raised effect is created not by weaving but by pressing and it may not be permanent.

Plissé. A cotton fabric crinkled by shrinking sections with a chemical. Used for lingerie and sleepwear.

Quilted fabrics. These fabrics usually consist of three layers of fabrics—the top fashion fabric, a layer of wadding filling and a backing. Naturally the resulting complete fabric is bulky and warm, and so is ideal for jackets and coats. Available in different weights in cottons, silks and synthetics.

Sailcloth. A member of the canvas family but in lighter weights. Available in solid colours and prints.

Satin. A shiny silk or synthetic fabric using the basic satin weave: that is, either the warp or filling has threads with long 'floats' (a thread which skips over or under several threads) running in the opposite direction.

Seersucker. A plain-weave fabric with permanent woven crinkle, available in striped, checks, and plaids. The crinkle can be an all-over texture on the fabric, or it can be arranged in 'stripes', narrow or broad, to form a pattern in itself.

Serge. A flat ribbed fabric, with the rib going diagonally from the lower left to upper right. Of wool, worsted, cotton or synthetics.

Sharkskin. Two types of fabric are known as sharkskin: one is a worsted suiting, generally in grey or brown, with a small weave design resembling the skin of a shark; the other is a somewhat heavy, semi-crisp summer sportswear material made of acetate, rayon or blends.

Silk. A luxury natural fabric. Various weights and types available: e.g. honan, a fine-quality wild silk; pongee, a lightweight fabric with nubs and irregular cross ribs; shantung, similar to pongee but heavier and rough; tussah, a coarse uneven light brown silk.

Stretch fabrics. Many popular fabric types and weaves have the additional feature of stretch. Included among these are denim, twill, gabardine and poplin. Those that stretch lengthwise are generally used for trousers; crosswise stretch goes into dresses, skirts, blouses, jackets and shirts.

Surah. A soft, lustrous fine twill of silk or synthetics in solid colours or prints.

Taffeta. A fine, crisp plain-weave fabric smooth on both sides and with surface sheen. Often used as lining fabric.

Ticking. Originally used for mattresses, ticking stripes now make smart sports suits and coats.

Tulle. A silk or synthetic net with a six-sided mesh. Used in layers for evening dresses.

Tweed. A rough plain or twill-weave fabric. Generally has contrasting slubs and nubs. Good for winter coats, suits and skirts.

Twill. There are various types of twill-weave fabrics. The basic twill weave runs up from left to right in a diagonal line. Variations include the popular herringbone (also called 'chevron') so named because it resembles a herring's backbone.

Voile. A light, semi-transparent fabric usually of cotton. In prints and plain colours.

Whipcord. A rugged, hardwearing fabric distinguished by a prominent upright slanted rib. A twill weave.

Wool. A natural fabric produced from the hair of sheep or lamb. Many kinds and weights available: e.g. Viyella, a lightweight fabric; Afghalaine, dressweight, soft and fine; velour, a heavier coatweight cloth.

Worsted. A fabric produced from yarn spun from combed wool. Generally considered as belonging to the wool family, though the original fibres are obtained from animals other than sheep. For instance, Angora and Mohair are produced from the Angora goat or rabbit; camel hair comes from the hair of the Asiatic camel; cashmere is from the hair of the Kashmir goat.

THE RIGHT NEEDLE AND THREAD

Whether you are sewing by hand or by machine it is essential you use the correct weight and type of thread for your fabric, and also the right needle size. There are good multi-purpose threads available which can be successfully used with all fabric types, but as a general rule natural threads should always be used with natural fabrics, and synthetic threads with synthetic fabrics. Using a cotton thread, for instance, with a nylon fabric can cause ugly puckering of seams, and when washing the garment the cotton thread might shrink slightly, whereas the fabric will not.

On the other hand if you use a synthetic thread to sew a cotton dress, when you come to iron the garment you will in all probability set your iron at a hot temperature to suit cotton—but this temperature could quite easily melt the synthetic thread which should only have a cool iron. The following chart gives a general guide to the correct thread and needle size for different fabrics.

Fabric	Thread	Needles Hand	Machine	Machine stitches per inch
Fine—net, organdie, lace, lawn, voile, chiffon, tulle	Natural: cotton 50 Man-made: Terylene	9	9–11	12–16 (natural); 12–14 (Terylene)
Lightweight—silk, gingham, muslin, poplin, seersucker, crêpe, taffeta	Natural: cotton 50 Man-made: Terylene	8–9	11–14	12–14
Mediumweight—tweed, wool, jersey, corduroy, linen, satin, brocade, velvet, suitings	Natural: cotton 40 Man-made: Terylene	7–8	11–14	12–14

Fabric	Thread	Needles Hand	Machine	Machine stitches per inch
Heavyweight-twill, canvas, duck, furnishing fabrics, foam-backed	Natural: cotton 36-40 Man-made: Terylene	6	16-18	8-10
Stretch fabrics	Terylene	Lightweight: 9 Heavyweight: 9	9-11 11-14	10-14 (use special stretch stitch)
Special fabrics-PVC, leather, suede	Terylene	9	16-18	6-10

WHAT SIZE AND SHAPE ARE YOU?

The key to successful dressmaking is to establish the right paper pattern size for your shape and size of figure. Of course patterns can be adjusted to allow for any personal idiosyncrasies in your shape, for few of us are exactly 'stock size', but if you start with a paper pattern which is as near as possible to your measurements, there will be fewer adjustments to be made, and the finished result should be more professional looking.

Commercial paper patterns are grouped under eight different types, and most figures fall into one or the other of these eight categories. Read the description of each category, below, and decide which one seems to be most like your own.
(**Note.** The names of these figure types are not descriptive of age. The types are based on height, body proportions and the contours of the figure. Thus some teenagers, for instance, will find that a Half-Size pattern fits them best; and there are adults whose measurements and figure proportions are best fitted by a Young Junior/Teen type pattern.)

Girls'. From 4ft. 2in. to 5ft. 1in. This is the smallest of the range of figure types. Because the bustline is not defined on this just-developing figure, no underarm dart is needed in the dress bodice.
Chubbie. From 4ft. 2in. to 5ft. 1in. This is for the growing girl who weighs more than the average for her age and height. Girls' and Chubbie patterns are the same height in comparable sizes.
Young Junior/Teen. About 5ft. 1in. to 5ft. 3in. This range is for the developing teen and pre-teen figure which has a very small, high bust with a waist larger in proportion to the bust.
Junior Petite. About 5ft. to 5ft. 1in. This is a short, well-developed figure with small body structure and a shorter waist length than any other type.
Miss Petite. About 5ft. 2in. to 5ft. 3in. This is a shorter figure than a Miss and has a shorter waist length than the comparable Miss size but is longer than the corresponding Junior Petite.
Miss. About 5ft. 5in. to 5ft. 8in. This is well-proportioned and well-developed in all body areas, and is the tallest of all figure types. This type can be called the 'average' figure.

Half-Size. About 5ft. 2in. to 5ft. 3in. This is a fully developed shorter figure with narrower shoulders than the Miss. The waist is larger in proportion to the bust than in the other mature figure types.

Woman. About 5ft. 5in. to 5ft. 6in. This is a larger, more mature figure of about the same height as a Miss. The back waist length is longer because the back is fuller, and all measurements are larger proportionately.

Taking your own measurements

To establish your exact figure type and size it is necessary to take your actual body measurements—these are the measurements of your own body at the specific points listed below. These are not the measurements of your pattern; a pattern always adds to the body measurements sufficient ease for movement.

When taking your measurements never be tempted to cheat by adding or subtracting inches where you would like them to be. Or to say to yourself, 'I am going to start dieting next week, so I'll allow for the inches I shall lose!'

Be honest with yourself about your figure as it is now. A garment which is made exactly to measure, whatever your shape or size, will look several times better than one that is made to the figure you would like to be.

If possible persuade a friend or member of your family to help you take your measurements. Ask her to write down the measurements as soon as she has taken them—then believe them! Be sure too that you take the measurements over the sort of bra and girdle you normally wear and are likely to be wearing for some time. Different foundation garments can add and subtract inches. Measure at the following points:

1. Bust. This should be taken round the fullest part of the bust, with the tape measure held well up at the back. Don't pull the tape too tightly or for that matter leave it too slack. It should just comfortably meet round your bust.

2. Waist. Place the tape round your natural waistline. Again do not pull it too tightly, and stand relaxed, without trying to pull in your tummy more than you would normally do.

3. Hips. Measure round the fullest part of your hips—this point is usually about 7–8in. down from your waist but it varies from one figure to the next.

4. Centre back to waist. Find the knobbly bone at the top of your spine and measure straight down from this point to your waistline. It is practically impossible to take this measurement without the help of a friend.

Finally write down your **height** without shoes.

Your figure type is based on two of these measurements: your height and your back waist length. If you are short-waisted with a well-developed figure, you will probably need a Junior Petite or Half-Size pattern. If you have a very young figure with a high, small or undefined bust you may be a Girls' or a Young Junior/Teen figure type. If you are tall, and have an average or long-waisted figure you may need either a Misses' or Women's pattern.

If you find two figure types that have the same bust, waist and hip measurements as yours, check the back waist lengths, and choose the type with the back waist length nearest to your own measurements. If your measurements fall between two sizes, select the smaller size if you are small-boned, or pick the larger size if you are large-boned or full-bodied.

If you are going to make a dress, blouse, suit or coat, select the size with the bust size nearest to yours.

If you are going to make a skirt, shorts or trousers, then select the size by the waist measurement. If your hips are much larger in proportion to your waist, then select the size by the hip measurement and alter at the waist.

If the pattern includes more than one type of garment, such as a mix and match set of blouse, jacket, skirt and trousers, then select the pattern by the bust measurement. If necessary adjust the hip measurement to fit.

Taking measurements for trousers
Stand evenly on both feet. Measure snugly over the under-garments you usually wear with trousers. Measure at the following points:
1. Waist.
2. Hip.
3. Thigh.
4. Knee.
5. Calf.
6. Round instep and heel.
7. Side length, from waist to desired finished length.
8. Crutch length—taken sitting down, from natural waistline to the top of the chair seat, then add on $\frac{3}{4}$in.

Taking children's measurements
Always buy children's patterns by size, and not by age. When measuring babies, take the weight and the height. If weight and height fall into different sizes, decide proper size by weight.

Children should first be measured round chest, taking the tape under the arms and over fullest part of chest at front and the bottom of shoulder blades at the back. Measure the child's height by standing him or her against a wall, without shoes.

Taking boys' and men's measurements
For coats and jackets, measure around the fullest part of the chest. For shirts, measure around the neck and add $\frac{1}{2}$in. for the neckband. For shirt sleeves, measure from back base of neck along shoulder to wrist. For trousers, measure around waist over shirt (not over trousers). Be sure to measure at natural waist as this determines size even if trousers are designed as hip-huggers. Measure hip round fullest part of hip.

MEASUREMENT CHARTS
As approved by the Measurement Standard Committee of the Pattern Fashion Industry.

BABIES

Age	Newborn (1–3 months)	6 months
Weight	7–13lb.	13–18lb.
Height	17–24in.	24–26$\frac{1}{2}$in.

TODDLERS'

Size	$\frac{1}{2}$	1	2	3	4
Breast or chest	19	20	21	22	23
Waist	19	$19\frac{1}{2}$	20	$20\frac{1}{2}$	21
Approximate height	28	31	34	37	40
Finished dress length	14	15	16	17	18

CHILDREN'S

Size	1	2	3	4	5	6
Breast or chest	20	21	22	23	24	25
Waist	$19\frac{1}{2}$	20	$20\frac{1}{2}$	21	$21\frac{1}{2}$	22
Hip	—	—	—	24	25	26
Back waist length	$8\frac{1}{4}$	$8\frac{1}{2}$	9	$9\frac{1}{2}$	10	$10\frac{1}{2}$
Approximate height	31	34	37	40	43	46
Finished dress length	17	18	19	20	22	24

GIRLS'

Size	7	8	10	12	14
Breast	26	27	$28\frac{1}{2}$	30	32
Waist	23	$23\frac{1}{2}$	$24\frac{1}{2}$	$25\frac{1}{2}$	$26\frac{1}{2}$
Hip	27	28	30	32	34
Back waist length	$11\frac{1}{2}$	12	$12\frac{3}{4}$	$13\frac{1}{2}$	$14\frac{1}{4}$
Approximate height	50	52	56	$58\frac{1}{2}$	61

CHUBBIE

Size	$8\frac{1}{2}$c	$10\frac{1}{2}$c	$12\frac{1}{2}$c	$14\frac{1}{2}$c
Breast	30	$31\frac{1}{2}$	33	$34\frac{1}{2}$
Waist	28	29	30	31
Hip	33	$34\frac{1}{2}$	36	$37\frac{1}{2}$
Back waist length	$12\frac{1}{2}$	$13\frac{1}{4}$	14	$14\frac{3}{4}$
Approximate height	52	56	$58\frac{1}{2}$	61

MISSES'

Size	6	8	10	12	14	16	18	20
Bust	$30\frac{1}{2}$	$31\frac{1}{2}$	$32\frac{1}{2}$	34	36	38	40	42
Waist	23	24	25	$26\frac{1}{2}$	28	30	32	34
Hip	$32\frac{1}{2}$	$33\frac{1}{2}$	$34\frac{1}{2}$	36	38	40	42	44
Back Waist Length	$15\frac{1}{2}$	$15\frac{3}{4}$	16	$16\frac{1}{4}$	$16\frac{1}{2}$	$16\frac{3}{4}$	17	$17\frac{1}{4}$

MISS PETITE

Size	6mp	8mp	10mp	12mp	14mp	16mp
Bust	$30\frac{1}{2}$	$31\frac{1}{2}$	$32\frac{1}{2}$	34	36	38
Waist	$23\frac{1}{2}$	$24\frac{1}{2}$	$25\frac{1}{2}$	27	$28\frac{1}{2}$	$30\frac{1}{2}$
Hip	$32\frac{1}{2}$	$33\frac{1}{2}$	$34\frac{1}{2}$	36	38	40
Back Waist Length	$14\frac{1}{2}$	$14\frac{3}{4}$	15	$15\frac{1}{4}$	$15\frac{1}{2}$	$15\frac{3}{4}$

*Top: the Singer luxury 760 sewing machine and,
below, an example of the edge stitching the
machine will produce.*

JUNIOR PETITE

Size	3jp	5jp	7jp	9jp	11jp	13jp
Bust	$30\frac{1}{2}$	31	32	33	34	35
Waist	$22\frac{1}{2}$	23	24	25	26	27
Hip	$31\frac{1}{2}$	32	33	34	35	36
Back Waist Length	14	$14\frac{1}{4}$	$14\frac{1}{2}$	$14\frac{3}{4}$	15	$15\frac{1}{4}$

YOUNG JUNIOR/TEEN

Size	5/6	7/8	9/10	11/12	13/14	15/16
Bust	28	29	$30\frac{1}{2}$	32	$33\frac{1}{2}$	35
Waist	22	23	24	25	26	27
Hip	31	32	$33\frac{1}{2}$	35	$36\frac{1}{2}$	38
Back Waist Length	$13\frac{1}{2}$	14	$14\frac{1}{2}$	15	$15\frac{3}{8}$	$15\frac{3}{4}$

WOMEN'S

Size	38	40	42	44	46	48	50
Bust	42	44	46	48	50	52	54
Waist	35	37	39	$41\frac{1}{2}$	44	$46\frac{1}{2}$	49
Hip	44	46	48	50	52	54	56
Back Waist Length	$17\frac{1}{4}$	$17\frac{3}{8}$	$17\frac{1}{2}$	$17\frac{5}{8}$	$17\frac{3}{4}$	$17\frac{7}{8}$	18

HALF-SIZE

Size	$10\frac{1}{2}$	$12\frac{1}{2}$	$14\frac{1}{2}$	$16\frac{1}{2}$	$18\frac{1}{2}$	$20\frac{1}{2}$	$22\frac{1}{2}$	$24\frac{1}{2}$
Bust	33	35	37	39	41	43	45	47
Waist	27	29	31	33	35	$37\frac{1}{2}$	40	$42\frac{1}{2}$
Hip	35	37	39	41	43	$45\frac{1}{2}$	48	$50\frac{1}{2}$
Back Waist Length	15	$15\frac{1}{4}$	$15\frac{1}{2}$	$15\frac{3}{4}$	$15\frac{7}{8}$	16	$16\frac{1}{8}$	$16\frac{1}{8}$

BOYS' AND TEEN-BOYS'

	Boys'				Teen-Boys'			
Size	7	8	10	12	14	16	18	20
Chest	26	27	28	30	32	$33\frac{1}{2}$	35	$36\frac{1}{2}$
Waist	23	24	25	26	27	28	29	30
Hip (Seat)	27	28	$29\frac{1}{2}$	31	$32\frac{1}{2}$	34	$35\frac{1}{2}$	37
Neckband	$11\frac{3}{4}$	12	$12\frac{1}{2}$	13	$13\frac{1}{2}$	14	$14\frac{1}{2}$	15
Heights	48	50	54	58	61	64	66	68

Note. For Toddlers' and Little Boys' (1 to 6) — See Toddlers' and Children's charts.

MEN'S

Size	34	36	38	40	42	44	46	48
Chest	34	36	38	40	42	44	46	48
Waist	28	30	32	34	36	39	42	44
Hip (Seat)	35	37	39	41	43	45	47	49
Neckband	14	$14\frac{1}{2}$	15	$15\frac{1}{2}$	16	$16\frac{1}{2}$	17	$17\frac{1}{2}$
Shirt Sleeve	32	32	33	33	34	34	35	35

More examples of stitching from the Singer 760 sewing machine. Top: a straight stitch that stretches with the fabric, and speed-basting embroidery. Bottom: decorative stitches, and blind hemming.

First steps

GETTING TO KNOW YOUR SEWING MACHINE

Before you can reach the exciting stage of buying fabric, cutting it out and making it up into an attractive fashion garment to suit and fit you, it is a good idea to spend some time just getting to know and understand your sewing machine. After all, this is the most vital piece of sewing equipment in your possession.

If you have still to buy your machine, then before spending a lot of money on an expensive sewing machine, consider carefully several points. First, what sort of sewing do you intend to do? If you want to do a lot of fancy decorative work then the machine you select will be quite different from a model capable of only straightforward 'plain' sewing—it will also cost quite a lot more.

Although there are many hundreds of models of sewing machines available, basically most of these fall into one of two categories: a straight-stitch machine, and a zigzag-stitch machine.

A straight-stitch machine sews only in a straight line, backward or forward, and is adjustable for length of stitch. Attachments are available which expand the usefulness of this machine, so if the initial cost is an important factor in your choice, the straight-stitch machine might be the one to buy. The zigzag machine is a different matter altogether. There are a great number of models in a wide range of prices. The best way to choose is to visit sewing centres maintained by the various machine manufacturers and try the machines under supervision. The more a machine can do, the more it will cost. When making your selection, remember you will be using the machine for many years.

Machines are available as console models, which are free-standing and permanently ready for use, with their own flat working surface. Portable models also of course have advantages as they are easy to carry around, to take from one part of the house to another, or—if you wish—to take with you when you go on holiday. Tables into which a portable machine can be set are available. Really a sewing machine is a very personal piece of equipment: so be sure to choose one which is right for you, for the sort of work you intend to do, and for your way of life.

Although nearly all the modern machines produced today are electric, many women are perfectly happy to continue using old manually-operated machines. Again, provided you know and understand your machine, there is no reason why you shouldn't produce as expert results from an old machine as you would from an intricate and expensive modern model. I am fortunate enough to own a portable machine made in the second half of the 19th century. It was bought for next to nothing in a junk shop, only does chain stitch, but does this very adequately indeed. I have used this machine extensively for plain sewing, for making fashion garments and soft furnishings for my home. The results are perfectly acceptable!

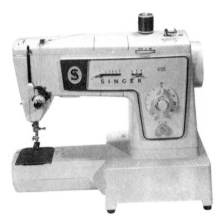

Remember however, whichever type of machine you choose, that a sewing machine is a precision instrument. It requires constant care and attention if it is to run well. The instruction manual will show how to keep it in good working order, how to make simple adjustments and how to operate it. If you do not have the manual for your machine, the manufacturer can usually supply one even if the machine is not of recent manufacture. It is well worth having the manual at hand constantly as a reference to the names of the operating parts mentioned from time to time in sewing directions. The manual will also tell you how to adjust the pressure and tension on your machine so your fabric is held firmly while the machine is stitching, and so you get a balanced stitch exactly the same on both sides of the fabric.

The manual will also tell you how to thread your machine, fit the needle and alter the length of stitch. As a general rule, the finer the fabric the shorter the stitches should be. Heavy, thicker fabrics need longer stitches.

The actual machining of a dress you buy ready-made takes a factory machinist only a matter of minutes—there is no reason why you should not eventually do the same.

If you have never used a machine before, have several

Three zigzag machines by Singer. From top to bottom: model 416, a lightweight machine with stretch stitch and automatic buttonholer; model 438, which has all the features of the 416 plus many decorative stitches; and the luxury 760 'Touch and Sew' convertible which offers instant, perfect sewing—simply at the touch of a button—and a 'magic' self-winding bobbin.

practice sessions on odd scraps of material before you embark on making a dress. Begin by sewing straight lines of stitches. Use a soft pencil to draw lines on your fabric scraps then stitch along these guidelines. Then try squares, zigzags and curved lines, working at different speeds. Then do the same exercises without pencil guidelines.

Once you are proficient on one layer of fabric, do the same stitches on two layers, pinning the layers together with the pins at right angles to the line of machining, and stitching $\frac{1}{2}$in. from edge of fabric. If your machine has a hinged foot you can machine over the pins but with a fixed or rigid foot you must take them out as they reach the presser foot otherwise you could damage the needle. You will find it easier to keep your stitching line straight if you watch the distance between the edge of the fabric and the right-hand side of the presser foot to see that it is always the same rather than watching the line of stitching and the needle.

Even if you are already used to machining, it is always a good idea before making up any garment to take two scraps of the fabric you are using, pin them together and machine a few lines — curved, straight and zigzag. Look carefully at the fabric and see if it has puckered on one or both sides. If both sides are puckered, then the tension is too tight and the stitch probably too small. Loosen the tension, lengthen the stitch (a lower number of stitches per inch) and try again. If only the under layer is puckered, your fabric is 'travelling' so it must be basted before you machine any seams; otherwise without basting, the under layer will always end up shorter.

This tendency of the under layer to 'travel' can on occasion be useful — for instance, when you set in a sleeve, machine the sleeve into the armhole with the sleeve underneath and the teeth of the machine will ease away the fullness of the top of the sleeve for you. Or, if you are stitching straight and bias strips of fabric together, place the bias strip underneath as it is more likely to stretch than the straight piece.

If you have a machine with lots of attachments, do practise with them until you understand how they all work. The instruction manual with the machine should tell you how to fit and use them.

Fastening threads

Secure threads at the beginning and ending of a stitched seam with one of the following methods:

Backstitching. This is done on many machines by simply moving a lever to 'reverse'. If your machine does not reverse, raise presser foot, keeping needle in fabric, turn fabric round, lower foot, and stitch back over the last few stitches.

Tie thread ends. Remove stitched fabric from under presser foot, and cut threads leaving 3-in. ends on fabric. Draw one thread through to wrong side of fabric, and tie both threads together with a flat or reef knot. Clip threads to $\frac{1}{8}$in.

Lockstitching. This method can be used on firm, heavyweight fabrics. Before you start to stitch the seam, hold fabric in place with the left hand so that fabric does not feed through the machine. Raise the presser foot slightly with the right hand while making three or four stitches very slowly. At the end of the seamline lockstitch the final stitch following the same procedure. Clip threads to $\frac{1}{8}$in.

CHOOSING YOUR FABRIC
AND YOUR FIRST PATTERN

If this is to be the first garment you have ever made, it is important to choose both pattern and fabric with care. An ideal pattern for a beginner is a simply-styled dress or blouse, with no complicated fitting techniques, and preferably without a collar to set in or sleeves. A princess line dress where bodice and skirt are cut in one piece, is preferable to a style where the bodice is joined to skirt along waist line.

Choose an easy-to-handle fabric to suit the pattern you have selected. Slippery materials and ones that fray easily can try the patience of the most experienced dressmaker. Cotton fabrics are all good for beginners. So are the cotton and wool mixtures,

This elegant dress would be a good pattern choice for a beginner, for there are no sleeves to set in, and the bias-cut skirt has no waistline fitting. Top-stitching adds extra fashion interest to bodice and neckline.

and fine Shetland wools.

A plain fabric which will not need lining is a good choice. If you want a printed fabric, then make sure the design is a small irregular one. Checks, stripes and prints with a large or regular pattern repeat are tricky, as they need careful matching at seams and edges.

Check your pattern measurements

When you have bought your pattern in the size nearest your body measurements, it is advisable to check certain of its measurements with your own to see if the pattern may need some slight alteration before you cut out your fabric.

You have already measured your bust, waist, hips and back waist length; write these measurements down and from the back of your pattern envelope fill in the corresponding pattern measurements.

Also you should take the following measurements and write these down:
1. Sleeve length, from shoulder to elbow.
2. Shoulder length, from neck to armhole.
3. Sleeve length, from elbow to wrist.
4. Centre front skirt length.
5. Centre back skirt length.

Now take these same measurements on your pattern pieces. Measure the front shoulder, for measurement number 2 above. You will quickly be able to see whether you need to make any basic alterations in your pattern at this stage.

CUTTING YOUR FABRIC

Before you can begin to cut out your pattern pieces from your fabric there are one or two important preparations to be made. First, you must make sure your fabric is thread perfect: this means a single thread of the fabric's weave should run across the cut or torn edge from selvedge to selvedge. The following methods can be used to ensure your fabric is thread-perfect:

1. Tearing. If the fabric was not torn off the bolt of material at the time of purchase, check to see if it will tear. About an inch from the cut end, clip one selvedge with scissors, tear firmly and quickly to the second selvedge, then cut through the selvedge. If the fabric tears successfully, then repeat the process at the other end. Cotton and synthetics, some wools and silks can all be straightened by tearing, but never treat the crosswise edges of linens in this way.

2. Drawn thread. Clip into one selvedge with scissors. Pick out one or two crosswise threads of the fabric with a pin. Grasp the thread with your fingers and pull gently, slipping fabric along the thread with the other hand. Cut along the pulled thread as far as you can see it clearly. If the thread breaks, cut along the line it has made until you can again pick up the end.

3. Cutting along a thread. When a fabric has a prominent thread or rib or a woven pattern such as a plaid or check, it can be used as a guide for cutting from selvedge to selvedge.

Most fabrics should have been treated to prevent shrinkage. But if your fabric has not had such a treatment, or if you are in any doubt it is best to preshrink the entire fabric length before cutting out.

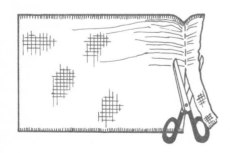

To shrink cottons and other washable fabrics, fold fabric lengthwise, pin selvedges and ends. Fold loosely several times. Put into warm water for about 20 minutes. Remove and unfold but leave the pins in. Hang straight over the bars of a clothes horse or several rows of clothes line. When dry, test to see if the grain of the fabric is straight. To do this, pin selvedges and edges of one end of the fabric together. If the fabric then lies flat and smooth on a table the grain is straight. If it is not absolutely straight, then pull the fabric gently on the bias (that is, crosswise to the grain of the fabric) in the direction opposite to that in which the off-grain crosswise thread runs.

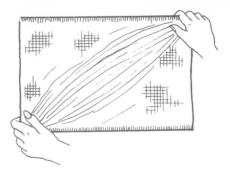

To shrink woollens, pin selvedges and ends together. Fold a large cotton sheet lengthwise and wet it thoroughly. Place fabric on the sheet so the sheet extends 6in. to 8in. beyond fabric. If necessary, use two sheets. Fold loosely and leave for 4 to 6 hours. Remove fabric and let it dry on a flat surface. If necessary, press.

Placing your pattern on fabric

Your pattern will include a number of cutting-out layouts. Choose the layout to suit the particular version of the pattern you are making, the width of your fabric, and the type of fabric (i.e. whether or not it has a nap or one-way design). Check to see whether your fabric is to be cut double or single.

If it is to be cut double, then fold it with the right side inside. If it is to be cut on a single thickness, then lay fabric on your cutting surface so the wrong side is uppermost. Now pin your paper pattern pieces carefully in position, following the correct layout diagram as given with your pattern. If some fabric pieces have to be laid on the fabric with a straight edge on the fold of the fabric this is to prevent the necessity for a seam at this point in the garment. You should therefore take particular care to place such pattern pieces accurately on the fold, with the piece absolutely straight.

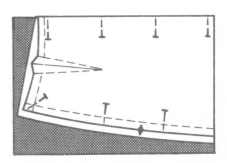

Pin these pieces in position first, pinning at 6-in. intervals along the folded edge and at right angles to it. Smooth out the pattern from the pinned line, and pin diagonally into the corners. Then pin the sides; set pins at right angles to the cutting edge, with the points always towards pattern edge. Do not let the pin points extend past the cutting edge. Pick up only a few threads of the fabric with each pin so the pattern will lie flat.

Pin the remainder of the pieces to your fabric, being sure to place them on the fabric grain as indicated by the grain symbol on your pattern pieces—this is usually a long line with arrowheads at each end.

Place the pattern piece so both arrowheads measure the same distance from the selvedge of the fabric. Pin first near these arrowheads, then smooth out pattern piece and pin round edges. Cut out all pieces with your cutting shears exactly along the cutting line. Cut with long, firm strokes never quite closing the shears. Do not lift fabric from the table; hold it down with the non-cutting hand.

When the same pattern piece is shown twice in the diagram— once in solid line and once in a broken line—the piece should be turned over before the second cutting.

When pieces are laid on a fold, such as a collar or a bodice

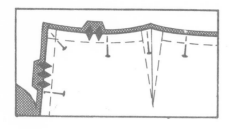

front or back, make a tiny snip or notch at both ends of the fold edge. This marks the centre point and makes it easier to match pieces accurately when they are joined.

When you come to notch markings on your pattern pieces (used to match edges of one piece against another), then cut little notches in your fabric, cutting the notches outwards from the cutting edge: this keeps the seam allowance intact. When there is a group of two or more notches all together, then cut these as a block rather than singly.

TRANSFERRING PATTERN MARKINGS

Your pattern pieces, as you will see, have a number of marks and symbols on them, as well as the basic information giving the umber and size of the pattern you are using, and usually the name of the particular pattern piece. All the construction symbols and marks—e.g. dart markings, buttonhole positions, pocket positions, indication of gathers—should be transferred to your fabric before you unpin the pattern piece. Straight grain symbols do not have to be transferred.

It is also a good idea to transfer the ends of seam lines to your fabric, and curved seam lines if stitching an even seam on curves is likely to be difficult. Straight seamlines do not have to be transferred. For darts, mark the stitching lines and the line through the centre known as the fold line. Mark a line at right angles to the point of the dart. This serves as a visible guide for the end of the dart when the fabric is folded for stitching.

There are various ways in which these marks can be transferred from pattern piece to fabric:

Dressmaker's tracing paper. This is used in conjunction with a tracing wheel. Use tracing paper in a contrasting colour to your fabric colour but light enough so the marks will not show through thin material on to the right side. To mark single thickness fabric, place tracing paper with its marking side against wrong side of fabric, place pattern piece exactly in position on top, then trace over all the symbols with the tracing wheel. Mark dots with an 'X'. Use just enough pressure to make a light line. To mark double thickness fabric, put one sheet of tracing paper face up under lower layer of fabric; place another sheet of tracing paper between pattern and upper layer of fabric. Trace as for single thickness method.

Tailor's tacks. With a long, unknotted double thread, take a small stitch through pattern and both layers of fabric, leaving a long end. Take a second stitch over the first, leaving a long loop. Cut thread, leaving long end. Cut through top loop. Remove paper pattern. Separate fabric layers. Clip threads between, leaving tufts of thread on both fabric pieces.

Chalk and pins. Place pins through pattern and both fabric layers on symbols to be marked. Fold pattern back, and mark alongside the pins. Turn fabric over and mark underside over the pins.

To mark the right side of fabric

Sometimes it is necessary to transfer marks on to the right side of fabric—for instance, for buttonholes or pocket positions. First, transfer the marks to the wrong side using any of the above methods. Then baste stitch over these markings on the right side.

Darts and seams

DARTS

Normally darts are the first construction detail you will sew when you begin to make a garment. The purpose of darts is to help mould the garment fabric over the body shape. This will give a neater and closer fit, and also help the fabric to hang nicely. Darts occur on a bodice front, to give shaping for the bust, on a back shoulder, at the waist of skirt, trousers and sometimes on the bodice as well for a close-fitting dress, on the elbow of a full sleeve, and, if there is not a dart on the back shoulder, then sometimes on the back neckline.

There are four principal types of dart: the straight dart, the curved dart, the double-pointed dart, and the dart tuck. In each case stitching may either be from the dart point to its wide end, or from the wide end to the point, whichever is easier. The point should be tapered to nothing, and there should be no 'bubble' at the end. After stitching is complete, tie the threads together in a neat knot at the point of the dart. Do not tie the threads so tightly that the dart point puckers. Curved and shaped darts are most easily shaped by pressing over a rounded surface such as a tailor's ham.

It is very important that you transfer the stitching lines accurately since some darts are straight, some curve out and some curve in.

Straight dart

This type of dart is normally used on a bodice front for bust shaping, on a back shoulder or neckline, and the elbow point of a sleeve.

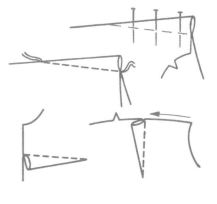

Working from wrong side of fabric, fold dart along centre marking line (usually indicated by a solid line on the pattern piece). Pin the outer marking lines (usually broken or dotted) together, matching any small dots. Pin with heads of pins towards fold of dart. Stitch along these marking lines. Continue with one or two stitches beyond the point of the dart, catching only one thread of the fabric along the fold. Press horizontal darts down, vertical darts towards centre of garment.

Curved dart

A simple curved dart which may be curved outwards or inwards, and is used often at the waist edge of skirts, trousers and bodices, is stitched in a similar way to the straight dart. Fold on the centre line and pin, then stitch along outer curved lines, following the curve marking carefully. Usually the dart is then slashed through the centre of fold and pressed open.

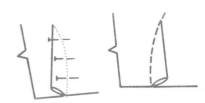

A shaped bias dart however is stitched in a slightly different way. This dart is either stretched or eased or is just so curved that it must be slashed first then pinned and stitched. This type

of dart occurs on an A-line dress; it starts at hip level and curves up to give a good bust fitting.

The centre line marking for this type of dart does not in this case indicate a fold; it is a slash line, and the dart is slashed along this line before being stitched.

First of all, however, to reinforce the dart, run a line of stitching down each side, just inside the outer marking line. Then slash along centre line, taking the slash exactly along the centre line, being careful not to slash beyond the line. On the wrong side of the fabric, bring the broken outer marking lines together and pin, carefully matching any small dots.

If there is ease or stretch it will be indicated on your pattern, usually between two medium dots. Ease or stretch the fabric so one side matches the other as you pin. Then stitch your dart. Sometimes it is necessary to clip into the seam allowance on this type of dart in order for it to lie flat.

Double-pointed dart

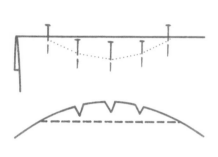

This type of dart normally occurs at the waistline of a fitted dress where the dress is cut in one piece for front and one piece for back, rather than separate bodice and skirt sections. Working from wrong side, fold dart along centre marking line. Pin the outer marking lines together, matching any small dots. Stitch from one end of the dart to the other, following marking.

Clip into fold of dart at centre point, and then once on either side of centre. Be careful not to snip stitching of the dart when you clip. Press dart towards centre of garment.

Dart tuck

This is a useful type of dart to give shaping to a bloused dress or shirt at the waist edge. It differs from other dart types in that its narrowest point is at the edge of the garment and it widens out as it is goes inwards towards the garment.

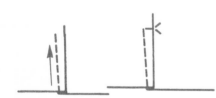

Working on the wrong side, fold dart on centre line and pin. Stitch along outer marking lines from the narrow end towards the wide end. When the wide end is reached, turn work in your machine and stitch straight across the wide end to the fold. Press dart towards the centre of the garment.

SEAMS

Stay-stitching

Although darts have been described as the first detail you sew in the construction of a garment, in fact this is not the very first sewing you do after you unpin your paper pattern from your fabric. Immediately after removing the pattern pieces, stay-stitching should be worked on all curved or bias edges to prevent these edges stretching during the construction of the garment.

This is simply a line of regular machine stitching made within the seam allowance (usually about $\frac{1}{2}$in. from the cut edge, if the seam allowance is $\frac{5}{8}$in.) through single thickness fabric. On deep curves, at necklines and waistline, stay-stitching is done on the seamline itself.

Stitching a plain seam

This is the most common of all seams, and is used for joining long straight edges together—e.g. for joining a dress front to the dress back along side edges.

Place the two edges to be joined together, with the right sides facing. Line up the edges exactly, matching any notches. Pin then baste along seam allowance. If your machine has a hinged presser foot for stitching over points of pins, then on a straight seam with an easy-to-handle fabric you need only pin-baste before doing the final stitching. Simply insert pins at right angles to the seam, with the heads towards centre of garment, and the pin points just touching seamline.

Check that your machine is at the correct tension and stitch setting for the fabric you are using, then stitch carefully along seamline. While the needle is stitching, guide the fabric only in front of the presser foot. This is usually sufficient to obtain smooth, even stitching. Sheer fabrics and fabrics with special finishes sometimes require additional support to avoid puckering. Hold the fabric gently with the right hand in the back of the presser foot without pulling while the left hand guides the fabric in front of the presser foot.

Curved seams should always be hand-basted first of all. Use a shorter machine stich than the one used for the straight seams. If you have a seam guide on your machine, then set this at an angle for curved seams so one corner of the end is in line with the needle. Guide the fabric edges lightly against the seam guide while stitching.

With very sheer fabrics, it is a good idea to sandwich a sheet of tissue paper between the two edges to be joined. Stitch seam, then carefully tear away the tissue. This helps to prevent puckering and 'drawing' in the seam.

If you are stitching a napped fabric to a plain fabric, work with napped surface up for pinning and basting, but have the plain fabric uppermost for stitching.

Seam finishes

Not only is seam-neatening essential to the look of a garment and its 'finish', but it prevents fraying and ragged edges, and gives a longer life to the particular garment. If you are going to line the garment, the seams do not have to be finished. There are various methods by which raw edges of seams can be neatened; choose the method to suit the fabric you are using.

Pinking. This is one of the easiest and quickest methods of all and is ideal for inexpensive, closely-woven fabrics such as cotton. All you have to do is to cut along seam edges with pinking shears after the seam has been stitched.

Machine stitching. This is a good strong finish for thinner fabrics like fine wool, linen, lightweight cotton and synthetics. After the seams have been stitched, turn under raw edge for about $\frac{1}{4}$in. and machine stitch close to fold.

Edge stitching. Good for fabrics that fray easily. After stitching the seam, make a row of stitching along each seam allowance about $\frac{1}{8}$in. from the edge.

Zigzag edging. If you have a swing needle or zigzag attachment on your machine, all fabrics can be neatened in this way. Just stitch along edges of turnings, adjusting the width of zigzag and length of stitch to suit the fabric. A loosely-woven material needs a deep zigzag, a finer fabric can take a smaller narrower one.

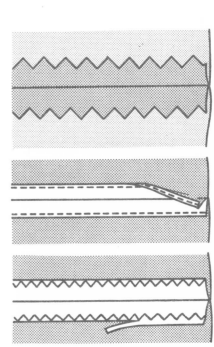

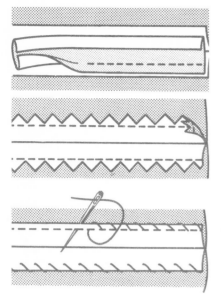

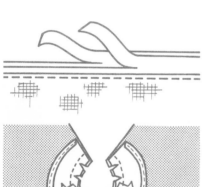

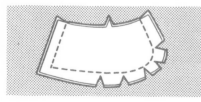

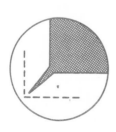

Rolling. Used chiefly on sheer fabrics. Stitch and trim a plain seam. Then roll the seam between thumb and forefinger and catch it to the seamline with small slanting stitches over the roll.

Bound edges. Excellent for loosely-woven tweeds or unlined jackets. Take a 1 in. wide bias strip of fine linen or silk to match the fabric, and stitch, right sides together, to the raw seam edges about $\frac{1}{4}$ in. from edge. Fold the strip over raw edge and machine stitch again along the seam close to the fold.

Stitched and pinked. This is suitable for a tightly-woven fabric because it adds stability to the pinked edge. Stitch $\frac{1}{4}$ in. from the edge of each seam allowance, then trim the edges with pinking shears.

Oversewing. This is the only method of seam finishing which should be left until the garment is complete. Trim the seams neatly, cutting away any loose threads, and then work small slanting stitches by hand over the raw edges. Work from left to right, or right to left. If the fabric is liable to fray, then a line of machine stitching should be worked first, $\frac{1}{8}$ in. from the edge of each seam allowance. Work the over-and-over stitches along the edge, inserting the needle just under the line of machine stitching. Keep the stitches fairly slack so the edge of the fabric is not drawn up.

Layering and clipping

The hallmarks of a badly-finished, unprofessionally-sewn garment are neck edges which refuse to stay in place, a frayed corner edge on a collar or front fastening, and a collar with a lumpy, bumpy edge. All these problems can be avoided if time and trouble are taken to layer and clip all curved edges.

Layering. Whenever two or more layers of fabric are seamed and pressed together—round a collar edge, neckline or armhole—the turnings should be 'layered'. This means each turning should be trimmed (after the seam has been stitched) slightly narrower than the previous one to give a series of 'steps'. When pressed, the edges will taper off smoothly into the garment without leaving a ridge.

Clipping. Except on very loosely-woven fabrics, the turnings of curved edges should be clipped as well as layered. This will prevent unnecessary bulk or lumpiness in the finished garment, and helps seams to stretch and lie flat. In the case of an inward curving (concave) seam, such as an armhole, all you have to do is to snip at intervals with small, sharp-pointed scissors into the seam allowance at right angles to the stitching line, but being careful of course not to snip the stitches.

For outward curving (convex) seams, such as collars, small notches should be cut at intervals from seam allowance. Again, be careful not to snip stitches.

Corners. There are two methods to help you achieve a clean-looking inner corner: you may simply reinforce the inner corner with a row of machine stitching, taking stitching about 1 in. each side of corner, then just clip to the stitching at the corner. Do not clip stitching.

Alternatively, if the corner is deeper and sharper, or if the fabric is inclined to fray easily, first machine stitch along the seamline, then cut a 2-in. bias square of matching fabric. Pin right side of this square to the right side of garment, centring it on the corner area. Stitch along seamline, including the square in the seam when you come to it. Slash garment and square evenly between stitching, just to stitching at inner corner (A). Turn the square to wrong side and press.

To achieve a sharp corner on an outer edge, such as a pocket, always trim outer corners diagonally before turning to the right side (B). This helps to eliminate bulk. With pockets and bands, when turning under edges before stitching in position to garment, turn under seam allowance diagonally just where the seamlines form corner (C). Then turn under edges on each side of corner.

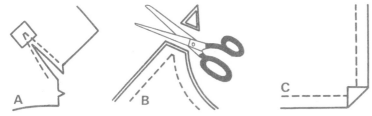

Seam variations

Eased seam (D). When one edge of a seam is slightly longer than the other the long edge has to be 'eased' to fit shorter edge. This type of seam often occurs at a shoulder edge. Hold the longer edge towards you, pin at intervals, matching any notches and also points where seamlines cross. Adjust the extra fabric evenly between the pins, and insert further pins so the fabric is evenly distributed across the edge. Stitch with the longer edge uppermost.

Top-stitched seam (E). Stitch a plain seam, press both seam allowances to one side. Turn garment to outside and stitch near seamline through pressed seam allowance. The term top-stitch may also be used to describe the stitching often done on the outside of a garment for decoration. This occurs frequently on men's shirts, for instance.

Double-stitched seam (F). Often used on tailored garments as a decorative finish or for reinforcement. Stitch seam and press open. On outside, stitch close to both sides of seamline.

Understitched seam. Used for attaching a facing to a garment. Stitch seam and press towards facing. On outside, stitch through facing and seam allowances. When facing is pressed to inside, the understitching also rolls to inside.

French seam (G). Used for underwear and on sheer fabrics. On outside of garment, stitch seam $\frac{1}{2}$in. from edges. Trim close to stitching. Press open. On inside, crease on stitched line. Then stitch far enough from crease to cover the raw edge.

Flat-felled seam. A useful seam for shirts and shirt blouses, and reversible garments. Stitch a plain seam either on the wrong side or on the right side, depending on which side you

A flat-felled seam gives a neat finish for shirts. On this sports shirt, the sleeve is set into the armhole with a flat-felled seam.

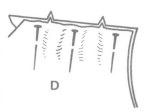

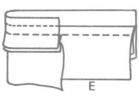

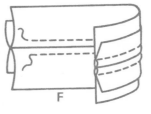

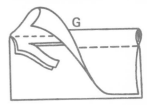

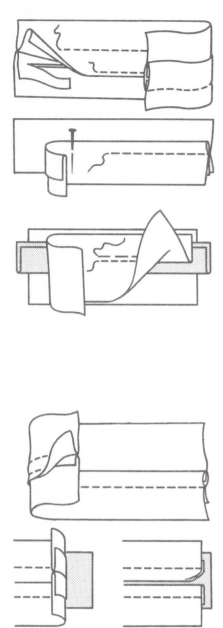

want the 'fell' to be. Press seam open; then press both seam allowances to one side. Trim the under seam allowance to $\frac{1}{8}$in. Turn under the raw edge of top seam allowance, and pin or hand-baste over the trimmed edge. Top-stitch close to the fold.

Lapped seam. Used for stitching yokes to garment, or where decorative stitching is wanted. Turn under seam allowance on top piece and press. Pin over the other piece, matching the seam edges, and top-stitch matching fold to seamline. Top-stitch close to fold, stitching through the three fabric thicknesses.

Taped seam. Used on front opening edges of coats and jackets, also on waistlines and other areas that might stretch. Unless tape is preshrunk, shrink it. Baste or pin to seam with one edge just over the seamline. Stitch tape and seam in one operation.

Piped seam. Used to give a decorative edge to collars, cuffs and faced necklines. Use a piece of ready-made bias binding or a bias strip of fabric, folding it lengthwise through the centre. Place the folded bias between seam edges with the fold overlapping the seamline, extending towards the garment. Pin, baste and stitch the seam. Press all edges to one side.

Corded seam. This is another decorative seam which can be used to edge collars, cuffs and necklines. Use ready-made covered cord, or cover a length of piping cord with a bias strip of fabric. Pin and baste the cording on the right side of fabric, matching the stitching of the cording to the seamline and with the corded edge facing towards the garment. Lay the other section right side down over cording, and pin. Stitch seam, stitching through four thicknesses of fabric, using a cording or zipper foot on your machine. Press all edges to one side.

Welt seam. Good for heavy fabrics wherever a strong flat seam is wanted. Stitch a plain seam. Trim one seam allowance and press the other over it. On outside, top-stitch about $\frac{1}{4}$in. from seamline. If wished, top-stitch again close to seamline.

Slot seam. This seam is used for decoration on blouses, skirts and suits of medium and heavyweight fabrics. Sometimes the fabric used under the seam edges is of a different colour to the garment fabric. Cut a straight strip of fabric the length of the seam and about $1\frac{1}{2}$in. wide. Mark lengthwise centre of the strip with basting or chalk. On the garment, press under the seam allowances, and baste turned edges to fabric strip so they meet at marked centre of strip. Top-stitch about $\frac{1}{4}$in. from edges, or at whatever distance is wished.

HEMS

Although it is normal to finish and stitch hems as the last stage in a garment's construction, the sewing of hems is in many ways related to seams and their finishing methods, so it is appropriate to include details of hemming techniques now.

Ideally, hems should be invisible from the outside of your garment, clean-finished and even on the inside.

First prepare your hem: have hem marked to length required; turn hem to wrong side on marked line, and pin. Try on garment to make sure the hem is even all the way round. Take off garment, and mark depth of hem—usually about 2–3in. is sufficient for a lower edge hem. Trim away excess fabric, being sure to trim away any loose threads. Neaten the raw edge by any of the seam finishing methods described on pages 31–32 (choose a method to suit the fabric you are using). Now stitch hem to garment, matching centres and seams, and using whichever of the following hem finishing methods is most suitable for your fabric and garment.

Catch-stitched hem. Press the hem well, then run the tip of iron under the neatened edge to take away any impression of stitching on the garment. Roll back $\frac{1}{4}$in. round neatened edge and very lightly catch the hem to the garment, using a single thread and sewing by hand. Pick up just a few threads of the hem fabric along the edge you have rolled back, and a single thread of the dress fabric. Space the stitches so they are about $\frac{1}{2}$in. apart, and leave thread loose between. As each stitch is worked let the hem fall back into position. This is known as catch-stitching, and is a useful stitching technique for catching facings round neck and armhole edges in place to the garment as well as for hems.

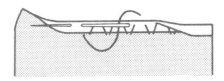

Bias seam binding hem. This is a good finish for heavier fabrics and fabrics that are inclined to fray. Lap seam binding $\frac{1}{4}$in. over the raw hem edge. Stitch close to the edge of binding. Slip-stitch other edge of binding neatly in place to garment.

Lace edged hem. Work as for bias seam binding hem, above, but substitute a strip of lace edging instead of bias seam binding.

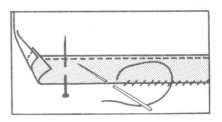

Rolled hem. Stay-stitch about $\frac{1}{4}$in. from the edge, and trim close to the stitching. Roll hem twice between the thumb and forefinger, making the width of the roll less than $\frac{1}{8}$in. Slip-stitch hem to garment.

Interfaced hem. Cut strips of interfacing 1in. wider than depth of finished hem required, and as long as required to go round the hemline. Place the garment wrong side up with the hem edge towards you. Pin the interfacing between the body of the garment and hem with the lower edge of interfacing $\frac{1}{2}$in. below the hem fold line. Use long stitches to sew the interfacing to the garment along the top and bottom edges. Take very short, shallow stitches in the garment, so that the stitches are invisible on the right side, and rather long stitches visible on the interfacing side. Fold hem to position and use a long running stitch to secure it to the interfacing.

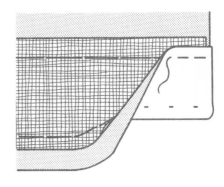

Eased or circular hem. Stitch $\frac{1}{4}$in. from raw edge of hem using a long machine stitch. Pin hem to garment, matching centres and seams. Ease in fullness by pulling up machine stitching. Press, shrinking out fullness. Finish with bias seam binding, as described for bias seam binding hem, above.

Pleat hem. A seam at the inside of a pleat is usually pressed to one side. About 1in. from top of hem, clip seam allowance almost to seam stitching. Press seam open below clip, and finish hem by any method wished.

Lockstitch hem. This is a good hem for garments which have to withstand hard wear, such as children's clothes. Work from left to right as follows: using knotted thread, on the garment side close to hem edge take a stitch through only one thread of the garment fabric. Directly opposite this stitch on the hem edge take another stitch, picking up two or three threads of the fabric. About $\frac{1}{4}$in. from this starting point, take a stitch through one thread on the garment side and then through the hem edge, passing the needle over the looped thread. Continue in this way.

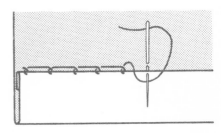

Sleeves, cuffs, collars and pockets

SLEEVES

Raglan sleeves and sleeves cut in one with the yoke of a dress or blouse are stitched in place using the various dressmaking techniques so far described. Raglan sleeves frequently have darts on the shoulder line. These are usually curved darts, and should be stitched and pressed open, following directions for curved darts on page 27. Sleeves cut in one with a garment yoke or with the front panel of a jacket or bodice should be reinforced at the inner corner of the underarm where sleeve and yoke meet with a 2-in. bias square of fabric (see directions for strengthening inner corners on pages 31–31).

Set-in sleeves demand a different set of sewing techniques altogether. This type of sleeve can vary from the full puffed sleeve often featured on a little girl's party dress to a full-length fitted sleeve for a winter dress or suit, to a short sleeve on a man's sports shirt. The principle however of stitching and setting the sleeve into the armhole of the garment is the same in every case.

A set-in sleeve should be free from puckers, should curve smoothly over the shoulder and hang straight.

Always take especial care to cut your pattern accurately— well-curved armhole edges will make sewing easier.

With nearly all sleeve types the sleeve invariably has more fabric round its top shoulder section, or 'head' as it is called, than the armhole of the garment. In order to fit the sleeve neatly into the armhole it is necessary to ease-stitch the top section of the sleeve before stitching it into the armhole.

Usually a pattern will have notch markings to show where the ease-stitching should be worked. Using a long machine stitch, make two rows of stitching between the notches on the sleeve, working first row exactly on the seamline, the second row $\frac{1}{4}$in. from the first row within the seam allowance. Leave about 3 or 4in. of thread loose at each end of both rows of stitching so the 'ease' can be pulled up to fit into armhole.

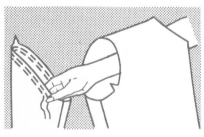

Stitch underarm seam in sleeve and finish lower (cuff) edge. Now the sleeve is ready to be stitched into the armhole of garment. First, have sleeve and garment with right sides out. Then, reach through the armhole of the garment from inside and bring sleeve to garment with right sides together. Match and pin seams at underarm. Turn garment over sleeve with wrong side towards you. Continue pinning armhole edges together matching all notches and marks, and placing the mark at the head of the sleeve to the shoulder seam of the bodice.

Ease in the fullness between notches on the sleeve by drawing up the loose threads on both rows of stitching until the edge of the sleeve matches the edge of the garment armhole.

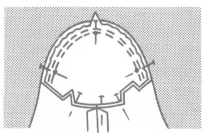

Distribute ease evenly each side of shoulder seam, but leave about 1in. at the top without ease.

Left: three-piece holiday outfit of dress, suntop and shorts, all from the same pattern. Right: pretty for a little girl—dress has a gathered skirt, square neckline and short puff sleeves; the apron is trimmed with embroidered eyelet edging.

Day and evening versions of the same pattern. Left: daytime version, with short sleeves, is made up in a soft wool. Right: long and sleeveless for evening, in a glitter party fabric.

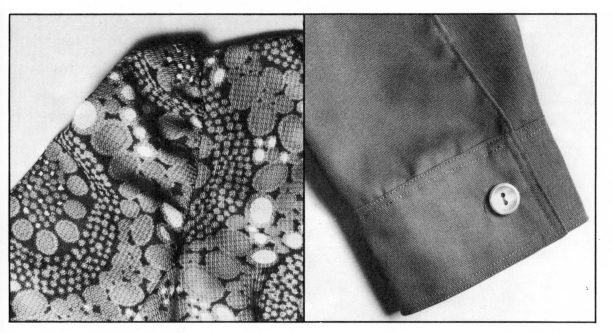

Now roll top of sleeve outward, shaping eased sleeve to armhole. Continue pinning each side of shoulders towards underarm and setting pins at about ¼-in. intervals. Make sure that raw edges are even. Ease lower part of sleeve (below ease-stitched top section) to fit into the armhole.

Baste, and remove pins.

Stitch along seamline with the sleeve side up, and starting at the underarm. In this way you can make sure that no puckers are caught in the stitching. When you have completed one row of stitching, work another row about ⅛in. from the first row within the seam allowance.

Trim seam close to second row of stitching round lower part of armhole. Leave upper (ease-stitched) part untrimmed.

Working from the inside, lightly and gently steam press the seam round upper part of sleeve, to shrink out the ease. Then turn seam towards sleeve.

Sleeve closings

There are three basic types of sleeve openings when cuffs are used.

1. Continuous lap. Stitch along marked stitching line at lower edge of sleeve, then carefully slash between the stitching. Slash right to the point but be careful not to clip the actual stitching. Open out and measure the length of the slashed edges. Cut a piece of garment fabric this measurement and 2in. wide. Press under ¼in. on one long edge.

With right sides together, pin strip to slashed edges of sleeve. Have bottom edges even, but pin the point of opening ¼in. from the raw edge of the piece. Place on machine, sleeve side up. Fold extra sleeve fabric out of the way and stitch ¼in. from edge of strip. Stitch again over first stitching to reinforce.

Press strip out away from stitching. On wrong side, pin pressed edge over seam and slip-stitch invisibly. Turn front lap to wrong side and baste to lower edge

Left: head of a gathered sleeve set smoothly into the armhole. Right: an example of a sleeve closing with cuff where an opening is simply left in the underarm seam.

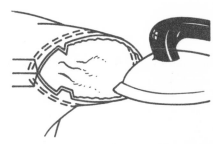

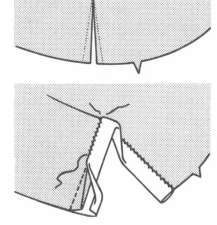

Dolman-styled dress has its wide sleeves gathered into tight cuffs.

2. Pleat construction. Reinforce the lower edge of sleeve by machine stitching along seamline, starting and ending stitching about 1in. each side of dot markings on the pattern. Clip seam allowance to the stitching at the dot markings but do not clip the stitching. Turn the seam allowance to the wrong side between clips. Turn under raw edge and make a narrow hem. After cuff is attached and fastened a small pleat will be formed at this point.

3. Opening in underarm seam. Stitch underarm seam of sleeve, leaving an opening at lower end of seam where indicated on the pattern. Turn $\frac{1}{4}$in. to the wrong side on seam allowance below the seam and stitch. Then press both edges to wrong side along seamline, and baste to lower edge. These edges will just meet after the cuff is attached and fastened.

Alternatively, press one edge to the wrong side along seamline; baste to lower edge. The front edge remains as it is, forming an extension. When the cuff is attached and fastened, the back laps over the front edge.

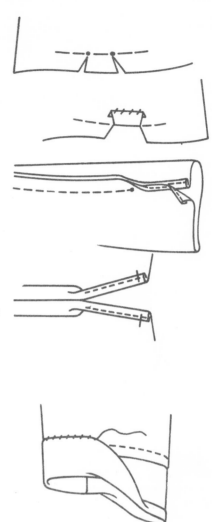

CUFFS

To make a simple, turn-back cuff, seam the ends of the cuff section together first, and press seam open. Press under seam allowance on one edge of cuff to the wrong side, and trim to $\frac{1}{4}$in. With the raw edges even, stitch the right side of cuff to the wrong side of the sleeve, matching the seams. Fold the pressed edge to the right side, and hem by hand along the seamline; press well. Fold the cuff to the right side of sleeve, catch to the underarm seam of sleeve with a few stitches.

To make a cuff with its own facing to attach to the lower edges of a gathered sleeve with opening, first cut interfacing section, if used. On the two outside corners of the interfacing trim diagonally $\frac{1}{4}$in. inside the point where the seamlines will meet. This eliminates bulk and makes it easier to turn the cuff to a sharp point. Pin interfacing to wrong side of cuff and machine baste $\frac{1}{2}$in. from cut edges. Trim interfacing close to stitching. Baste-mark buttonhole markings, if these are required. If you are making bound buttonholes, make them now.

Take cuff facing section. One long edge will most probably have notch markings in it. Press this edge to wrong side along seamline, and trim seam allowance to $\frac{1}{4}$in. With right sides together, stitch facing to cuff round other three edges. Reinforce the corners, as described on page 30. Layer the seams (see page 30), trimming diagonally across the corners. Turn cuffs right side out, working out corners carefully to give a good point.

With right sides together, pin the sleeve to the cuff matching any notches and underarm seam to markings on cuff, and placing sleeve opening edges at ends of cuff. Carefully adjust gathers in the sleeve so that the edge fits the cuff exactly. Tie ends of gathered threads and baste seam. With sleeve on top, stitch in place. Trim seam allowance to $\frac{1}{4}$in. and press towards the cuff. Pin the turned-under edge of cuff facing over the seam and slip-stitch neatly in place.

Turn sleeve right side out, then lap the front end of cuff over the back end. Pin carefully, making sure edges are straight. Sew button in place to correspond with buttonhole.

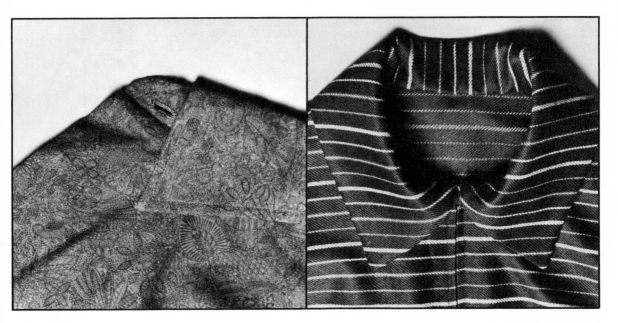

COLLARS

Although collars vary considerably in shape and size, they do in fact fall into three basic types: the shaped collar which lies flat; the straight collar which rolls; the straight collar which stands up. The basic construction details are the same for each type. Interfacing is used with most collars because the crispness and body which it adds improves the appearance of the finished collar.

Generally a collar consists of two sections: one will appear on top on the right side of the finished garment, and is known as the 'collar' (or 'top collar'); the other which will go underneath is the 'facing' (or 'under collar'). The interfacing is sandwiched between these two sections. First pin interfacing to wrong side of collar and machine baste $\frac{1}{2}$in. from the cut edges. Trim interfacing close to stitching. If you are making a collar with points, then before stitching interfacing to collar, trim the two outside corners of the interfacing diagonally $\frac{1}{4}$in. inside the point where the seamlines will meet.

Now pin the right sides of the facing section and the interfaced collar section together, matching any markings and notches. Usually one edge of a collar and its facing only has notches in it: this will be the edge which will be stitched to the garment neckline edge. Stitch collar and facing sections together along long edge opposite to this notched edge. Layer seam, and clip into seam allowance on curved edges. On inside, press seam towards collar facing. Then on the right side understitch close to seamline through the facing and the seam. With right sides together, pin and stitch ends of collar and facing together. Layer and clip seams, and trim corners diagonally. Turn the collar right side out, and gently push out corners with the point of closed scissors. A pin is also helpful in pulling out the point sharply.

Pin remaining open edge of collar and facing together, then baste. Your collar is now ready to be stitched into the neckline edge of your garment.

Double-breasted jacket, with shaped collar, has princess seaming, welt pockets and top-stitching detail.

Above: two examples of the shaped collar which lies flat.

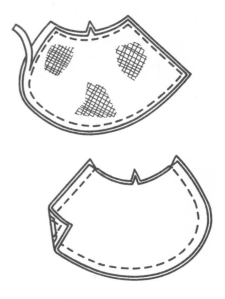

41

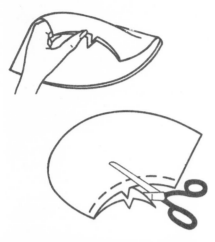

To make a successful round or curved collar which always lies flat, the secret is to roll and mould the collar into the shape it will be when worn before attaching the collar to the neck edge of the garment. After interfacing has been stitched to collar section, and interfacing has been trimmed, as for previous method, with right sides together stitch collar facing to the collar right round seamline on all edges except the neck edge. Using a tailor's ham or sleeve board, press collar seam open. Trim seam, clip curves and turn collar right side out.

Now on facing side of collar steam press, rolling the collar seam to the facing side. When rolling the seam to the facing side, taper from seamline at ends of collar. Seam should not roll to underside more than $\frac{1}{8}$in. With right side up, roll the collar over your hand moulding it into the shape it should be when it is worn. The notched (neck) edges will now no longer be even, as the collar facing extends beyond the raw edge of collar.

Place the collar on a table. The collar will most probably have a slight 'bubble' in it—this allows your collar to roll and shape properly. Trim away excess fabric from your collar facing on the neck edge. The collar is now ready to be attached to the neckline of your garment.

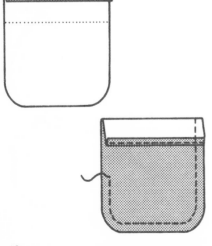

A simple, square patch pocket.

A few hints to help when fitting collars into necklines . . .

Always stay-stitch the neckline of the garment on the seamline. Clip the garment neckline before attaching a collar so collar seamline can be matched to neckline seamline.

Remember if you have altered the garment neckline to make it larger or smaller, you must also alter the collar.

After stitching and turning a shaped collar, fold it in half and check to make sure both ends are exactly the same length and shape.

POCKETS

There are three distinct categories of pockets: the applied or patch pocket which is stitched to the right side of garment in its appropriate position; the insert pocket which is placed in a seam of the garment; and the set-in pocket for which a slash or special opening is made in a section of the garment.

Of all these types, the patch pocket is by far the easiest to make and to position on your garment. Often a patch pocket can be added to a garment even though the pattern does not call for one.

The patch pocket

A patch pocket may be almost any size or shape—square, rectangular, curved at the lower corners, pointed at the centre of the lower edge, quite small for a child's garment, or enormous and capacious for a winter coat. Some are lined; some are finished with flaps. But whatever kind of patch pocket is involved, the general method of making and attaching to the garment is the same.

First prepare the pocket section by pressing $\frac{1}{4}$in. on upper edge to wrong side. Machine stitch close to edge. To form hem facing, turn upper edge to right side of pocket along fold line (do not press). Starting at top of hem facing, stitch around pocket on seamline. Trim upper corners of hem facing diagonally.

On a square pocket, fold the lower corners diagonally, exactly at the stitching and press. Turn hem facing to wrong side. Turn side and lower edges to wrong side along stitching. Press.

On a curved pocket, clip seam allowance to the stitching, or cut out tiny 'V' shapes. Turn hem facing and side edges to wrong side and press.

On a bias pocket (usually without a flap) to prevent stretching stitch both edges of a piece of straight seam binding to wrong side of pocket, just above the fold line.

If you want to line your pocket—and this does give an extra professional finish to the pocket—fold the upper edge of your pocket pattern piece along fold line; pin. Use this as a pattern for cutting lining section.

A patch pocket with buttoned-flap trim, stitched to garment just above the pocket.

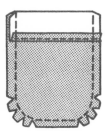 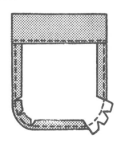 

Press ½in. on upper edge of lining to wrong side. Pin lining to lower part of pocket with right sides together and raw edges even. Turn upper edge of pocket down over lining along fold line, forming hem facing; pin. Stitch side and lower edges along seamline. Trim seam and corners. For curved pocket, clip curves.

Turn pocket right side out. Lap lining over facing and slip-stitch neatly.

Mark pocket line to right side of garment with hand-basting. Pin pocket along basting. Pocket can now be stitched to garment round side and lower edges. Work machine stitching close to pocket edge. If an 'invisible' finish is preferred, then slip-stitch pocket to garment working on right side of garment, picking up just a few threads of fabric on underneath of pocket with each stitch.

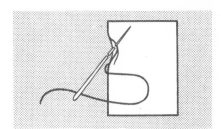

The insert pocket

This type of pocket is slightly more difficult to construct than a patch pocket but once you have mastered the technique, you will find it a useful method, often preferable to a patch pocket for elegant suits and dresses.

There are two basic methods of making an insert pocket:

Method 1: with extensions. With this method, extensions are added to that part of the garment to which the pocket pieces are to be stitched. The extension thus acts as a facing so the pocket itself will not be visible from the outside. It is therefore preferable to have the pocket sections of lightweight lining fabric as this will create less bulk than if the pocket were made from the garment fabric.

With right sides together, each pocket section is stitched to each extension, and the seams are pressed open. Then the two garment pieces and pocket pieces are placed together, right

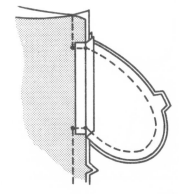

43

sides facing, and the garment seam and pocket seam all stitched in one continuous line. Reinforce stitching at pocket corners. If garment seam is to be pressed open, clip seam above and below pocket. Press seam open, and press pocket upwards front of garment.

Method 2: without extensions. If you are setting a pocket directly into a seam allowance without extensions, then it is best to have one lining section of the garment fabric, the other of lining fabric. Or if it is wished to have both sections of lining fabric, then sew a straight facing piece of garment fabric to side edge of pocket. Turn under $\frac{1}{4}$in. on inner edge of facing. Trim outer edges even with pocket—the facings are on the inside of pocket when finished. After seam in garment has been stitched, leaving opening for the pocket, stitch pocket pieces to each seam allowance, taking a $\frac{3}{8}$in. seam. Press seams towards garment. Sew curved edges of pocket pieces together, matching any markings.

Press garment seam open tapering seam allowance above and below pocket. Press pocket towards front.

The set-in pocket

A welt pocket is a good example of a set-in pocket, and not difficult to construct.

First baste-mark the length of the pocket opening in the desired position on right side of the garment. Next cut a straight strip of lightweight interfacing 2in. wide and 2in. longer than the opening. Baste to the wrong side of the garment under the marked slash position.

Right sides facing, stitch welt facing to welt leaving one long side open. Trim and clip seams, turn right side out and press well. Baste welt to right side of garment, with raw edges of welt just below the marked opening.

With right sides together, place one pocket section over the welt, having the top edge $\frac{7}{8}$in. above the mark for the opening. Baste, having the basting stitches directly over the baste-marked line for the opening.

Stitch $\frac{1}{4}$in. each side of this basting line, making the upper stitching line $\frac{1}{8}$in. shorter than the lower line at the ends. Be careful not to catch in the welt at the ends.

On the basting line, slash through the pocket piece only to within $\frac{1}{2}$in. of the ends, and from there clip diagonally into the corners. Then, keeping the seam allowance of the welt out of the way, make a similar slash along the marked line of opening on the garment through piece sewn under slash. Turn welt up and press. Turn the pocket piece to the inside through the opening. Turn welt up and press. On inside pin and stitch second pocket piece to the first one. On outside, stitch upper edge and ends of opening through garment and pocket. Slip-stitch ends of welt in place.

Fitting a pattern

Fitting is one of the most important keys to success in dress-making. It can make or mar a complete outfit. This is why it is worth taking time and trouble first of all to check your measurements honestly and accurately, and then to make any necessary alterations to your paper patterns.

Commercially produced paper patterns—just like ready-made clothes—have to be made to fit a standard, average-sized figure. But very few of us are exactly stock size in every respect! Once you begin to analyse your figure problems, you may well discover certain facts about your shape you may not even have been aware of before. For instance, you may realise why there are certain dresses or suits in your wardrobe—bought or home-made—which have never felt really comfortable. The reason probably is that they do not fit your particular shape accurately enough.

Fitting is not an easy or quick operation. It takes time and patience, for only one adjustment can be made at a time. It is very much a trial and error affair, and each adjustment may have to be made a dozen times before you get it exactly right.

THE TOILE METHOD

By far the most successful method of fitting is to make up your own personal toile, adjusted exactly to your shape and size. A toile, in case you have never met the term before, is a French word used by professional dressmakers to describe a calico shape. This shape is cut out, made up and fitted to show the exact lines of a finished dress or suit design, before the garment itself is cut out from expensive material. It is like a sort of master pattern which can be adjusted down to the smallest detail, until you are certain you have a perfect fit for your figure. Thereafter every paper pattern you buy is adjusted to the fitting of your toile, and no more time is wasted in fitting the actual garment. All the donkey work has been done on the calico shape.

Most paper pattern companies sell basic fitting patterns which can be used to make up your toile, but in fact any pattern for a simple classic dress would do. An A-line style of dress, with long sleeves and high round neck is best. Ideally you should make up separate toiles for a dress, a skirt, a blouse and trousers, to give a comprehensive coverage to all your fitting problems, but for a start a dress is quite sufficient.

Select the pattern size which is nearest to yours (see details for taking your own measurements, pages 14–15). If you are exactly halfway between two sizes, then select the larger size as it is nearly always easier to take in rather than let out a pattern. Suitable materials for making up your toile are calico, crisp cotton or muslin.

Alter the paper pattern for your toile first, then make up toile,

making final adjustments on it. Your toile should then be un-picked and the various pieces used as a master pattern for future dresses.

Never attempt to fit your toile, or any other garment for that matter, skin-tight. Once you think you have achieved a perfect fit, walk about and sit down in the toile to make absolutely sure it will be comfortable to wear. When fitting one side of the toile, keep an eye on the centre front and centre back lines and be careful not to pull them out of position. Do remember too that even once you have achieved a perfectly fitting toile or master pattern, your figure without doubt is changing all the time, and you must periodically check the fitting of your master pattern to make sure it is accurate. Only the most minor adjustment may be necessary, but this could make all the difference between a perfectly fitting finished garment and one which somehow just is not quite right, and does not justify the time and effort you have expended on making it.

ORDER OF FITTING
As with anything else, if you work to an orderly system, the whole job of fitting becomes easier. This applies whether you intend merely to alter an individual paper pattern or to make up a full-scale toile. The order of fitting in which you should work is as follows:
1. Shoulder darts and 'hang' of the back.
2. Shoulder seams.
3. Neckline.
4. Bust darts and 'hang' of the front.
5. Waistline.
6. Side seams.
7. Armholes and sleeves.
8. Hemline.

SHOULDER FITTING
A dress—or your toile, if you are making one—should hang in a straight line from your shoulder blades without any drag lines. The shoulder seams should run along the top of your shoulders, from your neck to the bone at the top of your arm. If this is not so, then identify your figure fault from the descriptions which follow, and make the necessary adjustments.

If you are round-shouldered . . .
your garment will pull up in the centre, and probably gape round the armholes. The shoulder seams will tend to fall to the back of your shoulder, instead of exactly along the top.
What to do: draw a straight line across pattern below the shoulder dart from the centre back to the armhole seamline. Cut pattern on this line; place tissue paper under cut edges. Separate edges the amount needed. Pin or tape to paper. Draw new cutting line from lower cut edge to the neckline. Straighten neckline curve. Make a neckline dart to take up the amount added to the outside edge, and make the shoulder dart slightly shorter.

If the pattern has a neckline dart (instead of a shoulder dart) then make neckline dart a little shorter, and add a shoulder dart to take up the amount added to shoulder seam.

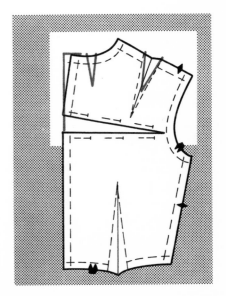

If fitting adjustments can be made on a basic master pattern such as this, then you should have no trouble fitting your garments.

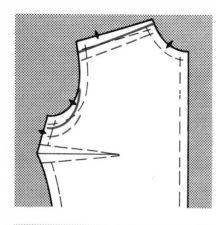

If you have sloping shoulders . . .

your garment will drag from the neck point to the underarm on both front and back.

What to do: measure the excess amount down from the shoulder line at the armhole. Measure down the same amount at the lower end of the armhole, and draw a new armhole curve to link these points. Draw a new shoulder line, tapering from the neckline to the armhole edge. Treat back and front of pattern in a similar way.

If you have square shoulders . . .

your garment will drag from the shoulder across the neck.

What to do: place tissue paper under shoulder and armhole of bodice front. Pin pattern to the tissue paper, or stick with strips of self-adhesive transparent tape. Mark the amount needed above the shoulder line at armhole end. Mark the same amount above the bottom of armhole. Draw a new shoulder line, tapering from neckline to armhole edge, and draw a new armhole curve. Treat the back in a similar manner.

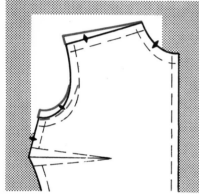

If you have lopsided shoulders . . .

and this is a fairly common figure fault, for few figures are exactly symmetrical—you will see a drag line towards the higher shoulder and the chest line will also be tilted up. Pull this shoulder down, or lift the other one up, then the drag line should vanish and the chest line level up.

What to do: adjust one side of your pattern only, following the appropriate instructions as given for previous figure faults. For instance, if you are adjusting the higher shoulder, then this will mean sloping the shoulder seam upwards from neck into seam allowance at armhole edge; if you adjust the lower shoulder, slope seam down towards armhole edge. A word of warning about lopsided figures in general: you will probably find other occasions when one side of your figure does not exactly match the other. Try, however, to keep lopsided corrections to a minimum as these could over-emphasise the lopsidedness rather than disguise it.

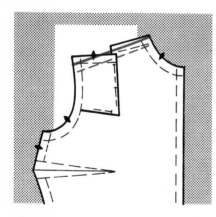

If you have narrow shoulders . . .

the seamline of the armhole will fall off at the shoulder.

What to do: on both front and back patterns, draw a line about 5in. long, starting at the centre of the shoulder line. Continue the line horizontally to the armhole seamline above. Cut the pattern on this line. Lap the cut edges the required amount at shoulder. Pin or tape to tissue paper. Draw a new shoulder line, and a new cutting line. Treat back and front in a similar manner.

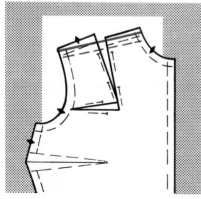

If you have broad shoulders . . .

there will be strain across the shoulders.

What to do: on both front and back pattern pieces, draw a line about 5in. long starting at the shoulder line. Continue the line horizontally to the armhole seamline. Cut the pattern on this line. Place tissue paper under the cut edges. Separate edges at shoulder line the required amount; pin or tape to the paper. Draw a new cutting line between neckline and armhole. Treat back and front in a similar manner.

NECKLINE FITTING

A neckline fits correctly when it lies at the base of the neck with no pull or wrinkles in the bodice. Very often the fault is merely in insufficient clipping of the curved neckline seam—be sure to clip the neckline seam to the stay-stitching at frequent intervals right round the seam. Wrinkles will often disappear when the neckline is properly clipped. A neckline will also fit better if the shoulder seam is stitched only to within $\frac{5}{8}$in. of the neckline, to the point where the neckline seam crosses the shoulder seam.

If the neckline wrinkles or strains at the front and back . . .

What to do : most probably the neckline needs to be lowered at front and back. Adjust by the appropriate amount, and if necessary adjust shoulder seams too—really this alteration can only be made on a toile or trial garment. Open the shoulder seams from the neckline almost to the armhole edge, and clip into and beyond the seam allowance round neckline curves. Adjust until neckline lies comfortably and flat. Draw in new neckline on front and back pieces, and starting at neckline pin shoulder seam together.

If the neckline is too loose . . .

it probably needs raising.
What to do : chalk in a new neckline above stitching line in the seam allowance.

If the front neckline stands out . . .

but the back lies flat, then front needs adjusting at shoulder seams.
What to do : reposition front shoulder edges so they fractionally overlap back shoulder seam at armhole edges. Repin shoulder seams in new position.

If the back neckline stands out . . .

but the front lies flat, then back needs adjusting at shoulder seams.
What to do : reposition back shoulder edges so they fractionally overlap front shoulder seam at armhole edges. Repin shoulder seams in new position.

BUST FITTING

The purpose of bust darts is to take in exactly the right amount of fabric at the side seams for your size bust, and the dart should taper away to nothing to finish about 1in. from the point of your bust. If your patterns are correctly fitted, your garments will hang smoothly down from your bust without drag lines or any surplus folds.

If you have a small bust . . .

there will be extra fullness at the bustline because the darts are too deep and the waistline too long.
What to do : decrease the width of the underarm and waistline darts the necessary amount to fit properly. Mark a new waistline seam from the waistline dart out to the underarm seam. Draw a new underarm cutting line.

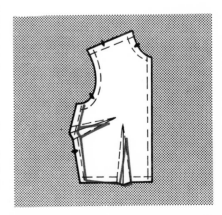

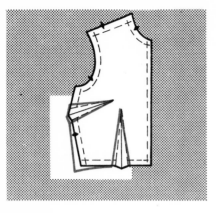

If you have a full bust . . .

tightness will occur across the bust and at the back of the bodice. The waistline may rise at the sides.

What to do: make the underarm and waistline darts deeper. Move the underarm seamline out slightly from bottom of dart to waistline. Slant the waistline seam downward from the dart to the edge of the pattern.

If you have a very full bust . . .

the waistline of the bodice is drawn up out of line across the front. Movement is restricted across the bust and back.

What to do: draw a vertical line through centre of waistline dart up to the shoulder line. Draw a horizontal line through centre of underarm dart straight across to the centre front. Cut on the horizontal line from centre front to the underarm seam. Place tissue paper under pattern. Separate pattern at centre front by half the total amount required to enlarge. Pin along the centre front edge, keeping the edges in a straight line. Cut on the vertical line from waistline to shoulder seam.

At bottom edge of upper side section, separate the pattern edges by half the amount needed to enlarge. Pin or tape these edges to paper. Where the vertical and horizontal slashes meet, separate the lower side from the upper section the same amount as at centre front. The vertical slash will taper. Re-draw dart lines. If amount added is great, make two darts instead of one at waistline.

If the bust dart does not point to the fullest part of bust . . .

the dart must either be raised or lowered.

What to do: to raise the dart, on the pattern front measure up from the dart point the amount needed to be raised and mark it. Draw new dart lines from the underarm seam to the new point on the top and bottom. Extend the point of the waistline dart the same amount that the underarm dart was raised.

To lower the dart, on the pattern front measure down from the dart point the amount it should be lowered, and mark it. Draw the new dart lines on the top and bottom from the underarm seam to the new point. Lower the point of the waistline dart by the same amount that the underarm dart was lowered.

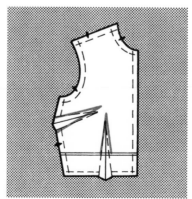 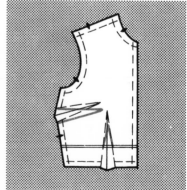

WAISTLINE FITTING

If you are long-waisted . . .

the waistline of the garment will fall above the natural waistline. Make adjustments on the front and back pattern pieces—most commercial paper patterns have a lengthening or shortening line printed on them to make waist adjustments easier.

What to do: if there is no line on your pattern, draw in a line about 1in. above the indicated waistline. Cut the pattern apart on the line. Place tissue paper under the two edges and spread pattern the necessary distance apart. Keep the centre front edges of the pattern straight and the cut edges parallel. Pin or tape pattern to the tissue paper. Complete the dart, seam and cutting lines.

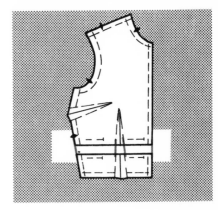

If you are short-waisted . . .

the bodice of your garment will be too long. This may cause wrinkles to form around the bodice.

What to do: if your pattern does not have an adjustment line printed on it, then draw in a line as described for long-waisted adjustment, above. Measure up from the line the amount needed to be shortened. Draw a line across the pattern. Fold pattern on the first line and bring the fold up to meet the second line, keeping centre front edge straight. Pin or tape the fold flat. Place paper under pattern at bottom corner; pin or tape pattern to the tissue paper. Draw a new cutting line and straighten the darts as necessary.

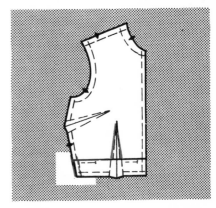

If you have a large waistline . . .

the extra amount needed can be added to the side seams and front and back of the bodice and skirt. If the waistline is quite a bit larger than the pattern, width should be added at the darts as well as the side seams.

If you have a small waistline . . .

divide the total amount to be decreased by four and remove from side seams of skirt and bodice, tapering seam allowance to meet original seamlines at armhole and hipline.

SIDE SEAM FITTING

Side seams are comparatively easy to adjust. If it is necessary to increase or decrease the entire side seams, then merely draw in a new seamline to give new side seam required on entire pattern length for skirt and bodice.

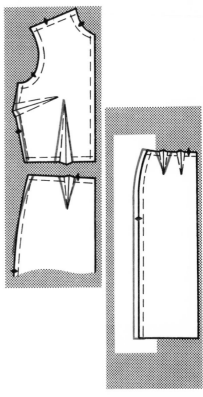

If it is necessary to increase side seams at one particular point only—at hipline for instance—then mark in extra width required at this point, then draw in new seamline keeping the extra width required even right up to waistline, and down to hemline. The waistline is then restored to its original size by increasing the width of the dart nearer the side seam by the same amount that was added to the side seams. Never try tapering the side seam back to the original waistline as this will distort the grain of the fabric, and only over-emphasise large hips.

SLEEVES AND ARMHOLE FITTING

When you are making adjustments in a sleeve pattern, it is important to keep the original shape of the sleeve cap, if at all possible. If the original shape cannot be retained, ease the extra fabric evenly when setting the sleeve into the armhole. Many sleeve adjustments are made in conjunction with bodice adjustments.

If you have a large arm . . .

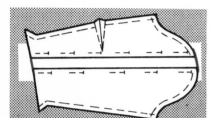

your sleeves will always be uncomfortably tight.
What to do: draw a line from the shoulder point on the sleeve pattern to the wrist, keeping the line parallel with the grainline indication. Cut pattern apart on this line. Pin or tape cut edge of sleeve front to tissue paper. Lay cut edge of sleeve back on paper the required distance from edge of sleeve front, keeping edges parallel. Pin or tape to paper.

On front and back bodice increase the armhole at side seam by adding half the amount added to the sleeve, then taper the cutting line to waistline.

If you have a thin arm . . .

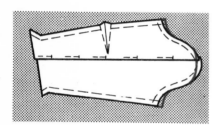

then your sleeves will always be loose and badly-fitting.
What to do: draw a line from shoulder to wrist on sleeve pattern, as described for large arm adjustment, above. On this line make a tuck of the required depth. Pin or tape. At the underarm seam in both the front and back, raise curve by half the amount taken up in the pleat. Draw in new cutting lines at upper edge and underarm seams. On the front and back bodice patterns, take off from the side seams at the underarm half the amount of the tuck in the sleeve, tapering to nothing at waistline. Draw a new line and raise the underarm as for the sleeve.

HEMLINE FITTING

This is the easiest fitting adjustment of all. Most commercial paper patterns have lines printed on them to indicate where to lengthen or shorten a hemline. If you are using a pattern without a printed line, then merely add to or subtract from the length at the lower edge. On some skirts, such as those having released pleats at the hemline, in order not to change the proportion, it is better to lengthen or shorten at the hipline. If your pattern has no adjustment line marked on it, then draw one in about 7in. below the waistline and lengthen or shorten at this line, following the instructions for lengthening and shortening a bodice pattern piece (see page 51).

A wardrobe of separates from a single pattern. The skirt has pleats at the front, is plain at the back. The trousers have turn-back cuffs and front zip fastening. Waistcoat is lined and has a back-buckled belt. The blazer is also lined and has patch pockets, back vent and long set-in sleeves.

Fastenings

A garment without some form of fastening could never be in any sense a 'fitted' garment, for a fastening—be it hook and eye, press stud, zipper or buttons—forms an important integral part of a garment design. Normally hooks and eyes, press studs and zippers are used for centre back fastenings on dresses, and left-hand side seam fastenings on skirts where a concealed fastening is required. Buttons are used where decorative visible fastenings are desired, such as on jacket and blouse fronts. Other more decorative forms of visible fastenings include rouleau loops and Chinese ball buttons made from bias strips of fabric.

ZIPPERS

These are probably the most widely used form of fastening for dresses, skirts, blouses and trousers. An ill-fitting and badly-sewn zipper can ruin the whole look of a garment, so it is worth taking time and trouble to learn the correct way to insert a zipper to your finished garment, whether by hand or by machine.

Machine-sewn zipper

The following method is suitable both for skirts and for dresses.

Working on the right side of garment, baste and press the seam allowance on the left-hand side of the zipper opening. Do not pull or stretch the fabric as this can cause one side of the opening to become longer and therefore unmanageable.

Working with the garment right side up on a flat surface, place the right side of zipper face downwards with $\frac{1}{4}$in. of the tape extending beyond the finished line of bodice or skirt, and the teeth $\frac{5}{8}$in. away from the raw edge. Pin and baste in place. The zip must be of the correct length for the opening, and should lie absolutely flat on the fabric.

On reaching the end of the zipper, allow the end of tape to slip to other side of seam opening. Baste and machine stitch with the zipper foot in your machine to the end of the tape.

When using towelling or bouclé type fabrics, machine stitch about $\frac{1}{8}$in. away from the teeth of the zipper, as these fabrics have a tendency to catch.

You have now inserted the right-hand side of the zipper. Remove basting and press well. Cover the zipper with a suitable pressing cloth to prevent shine marks and also if using a synthetic zipper.

Beginning from the lower end of the zipper, bring the left edge over the teeth and fabric $\frac{1}{8}$in. only, pin in position, starting $\frac{1}{2}$in. away from the end. Do make sure that you do not have a pleat or bulk. Now start from top of work, matching the edges and overlap $\frac{1}{8}$in. all the way along, pinning every 3 or 4in. Baste. Remove pins. Stitch by machine. Finally press for a perfect finish.

Smock dress with contrast neck tie is flattering for all figure types—making instructions on page 150.

Hand-sewn zipper

Fabrics such as soft wools, silks, sheers and knits lend themselves to this application which is not only less conspicuous but more flexible than machine-stitching.

For either the centred or lapped application, apply zipper to your garment as instructed for machine-sewn zipper, above, or as instructions given with the zipper. Do not, however, do the final machine-stitching which will show on the right side on your garment.

For the lapped application, the edge that is hidden under the lap may be machine stitched. For centred application, both sides should be hand-sewn.

Detail of a fly-front trouser zipper.

To hand-sew zipper, use a fine needle, matching sewing thread and a neat back stitch. It may be easier if you first make a row of basting on the right side of your garment where the hand-sewing is to be done. When basting, follow guideline on zipper tape or measure from the opening edge. For a lapped application, this should not be more than $\frac{3}{8}$in.; for a centred application, not more than $\frac{1}{4}$in.

Starting at lower end of zipper and working with a single strand of thread, bring needle up from the wrong side through zipper tape to right side of garment. Start sewing at the seam and either stitch a square across the bottom of the zipper, or form a point at the lower end. Alternatively for a separating zipper just start stitching straight into the long seam up side of zipper.

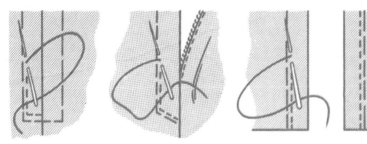

Take a very small back stitch, picking up just one or at the very most two threads of the garment fabric. Bring needle up through tape and fabric to right side, about $\frac{1}{4}$in. from the first back stitch. Continue in this manner the length of the zipper in an even line. On right side of garment there will be spaces between the stitches. The stitches will not touch each other as in the regular back stitch.

However, on the wrong side the stitches will be long and will overlap each other. This is a very strong stitching method.

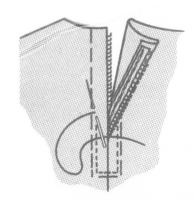

Sewing a zipper into a fly-front trouser opening

Turn top ends of zipper tape to right side. Keep both the zipper and trousers front right side up, and pin edge of left-hand front to zipper tape with the fold close to zipper teeth, placing the top stop $\frac{1}{4}$in. below waistline edge. Baste along fold, and machine-stitch, using the zipper foot on your machine. Continue to work with the right side up. Lap right-hand front over left-hand front. Match centre front lines and baste. Pin stitching line on right-hand front to zipper tape. Baste along stitching line.

Top-stitch fly front. At the bottom of zipper, starting at

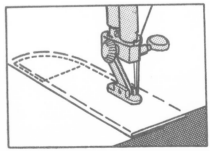

Shirt-style jacket for casual wear, with front zipper closing and shaped, bias patch pockets.

Pierced buttons will lie smoothly in place if a thread shank equal to the thickness of the garment fabric is provided.

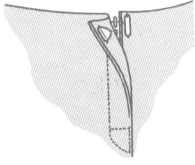

stitching line, stitch across to the opening edge. Pivot, and stitch along edge for about 1in. Pivot again, and stitch along basted line up to the waistline edge.

BUTTONS

There are basically two types of buttons: the pierced variety with holes in them, and the shank variety. For pierced buttons a thread shank must be provided if they are to stay in position and not distort the garment.

The length of the shank should equal the thickness of the garment at the buttonhole. If it is shorter, awkward pulling wrinkles will form, and if it is too long the garment will hang open slightly. It is mistaken thinking to believe that a button should be anchored to the fabric to be secure.

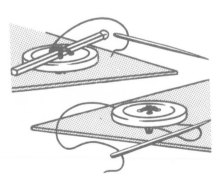

To make the thread shank, bring needle and thread to the right side of the fabric, and take a small stitch to secure the thread and the knot. Bring the needle through the button and place a toothpick or matchstick across the top of the button to allow for the shank, then bring needle through button again and back into the fabric.

Continue sewing back and forth over the matchstick. Remove matchstick and pull button up, forming a shank between button and fabric. Wind thread firmly around the shank. Draw the needle to the wrong side of fabric and fasten with several stitches.

Pin the garment closed as if it were buttoned to find the right position for the buttons. Place a pin at the outer end of the buttonhole into the fabric underneath. The centre of the button is placed at this point.

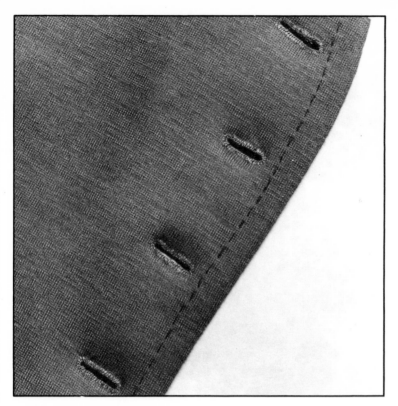

For a pleasing appearance the button should be 'framed' with fabric. That is, it should not be too close to the edge—about half the diameter of the button from the edge is standard.

The button should be reinforced if it is under strain or if the fabric is fragile such as leather and suede, plastic or a loose weave. Place a small flat button or a small square of firm fabric on the inside of the garment and stitch through it as you stitch on the button.

When a button is an unusual shape or a very rough texture, it may damage the fabric around the buttonhole. In this case, sew the buttons to the end of the buttonhole but do not finish the underside of the buttonhole. Then close the garment with covered press studs stitched right under each button.

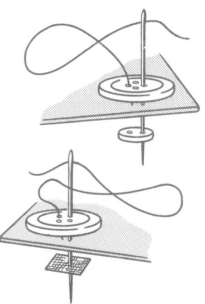

BUTTONHOLES

Buttonholes are usually $\frac{1}{8}$in. longer than the width of the buttons you wish to use. There are however certain exceptions to this rule. When very small buttons are used, the difference should be less than the $\frac{1}{8}$in., when a thick or heavyweight fabric is used for a coat and the button is covered with the same fabric, or the button has a high design (such as a ball button), the buttonhole should be slightly larger than the $\frac{1}{8}$in. difference. It is best always to make a test buttonhole of the same fabric as your garment before embarking on the finished buttonholes.

There are two principal methods of making buttonholes: the bound buttonhole and the hand-worked buttonhole. As a rule, the hand-worked buttonhole is used for shirts, blouses and lightweight dresses; a bound buttonhole for heavier weight dresses, for suits, jackets and coats.

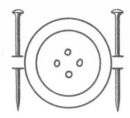

Hand-worked buttonhole

Place button on right side of fabric, the correct distance from the centre edge. This position should be marked on your paper pattern, and should have already been transferred to your fabric. Measure width of button and then add on $\frac{1}{8}$in.

Measure and baste along grain of fabric the width of the button plus $\frac{1}{8}$in. Baste $\frac{1}{8}$in. away from centre line above and below horizontal line to form a rectangle; curve the end nearest the centre edge of the garment.

Cut along centre basted line and oversew raw edges of fabric. Now work buttonhole stitches over the overcast edges, working from right to left as follows:

Start at end and insert needle into slit bringing it out below stitching. Bring thread from needle eye around and under needle point, from right to left. Draw needle up to form a 'purl' on the edge. Do not pull the thread tightly. Continue in this way, placing stitches close together so purls will cover the edge. At end towards garment edge, form a fan as shown in diagram, keeping the centre stitch of the fan in line with the cut. Make a bar at the end opposite the fan by taking several stitches across the end and working blanket stitch over the threads and through the garment cloth.

To finish, baste edges lightly together, press and remove basting stitches.

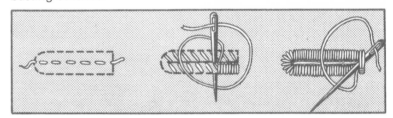

Bound buttonhole

Carefully machine-baste—or hand-baste for delicate fabrics— a vertical line at each end of buttonhole marking. Then baste a horizontal line along buttonhole marking, extending line by $\frac{1}{2}$in. at each end.

Cut a piece of organza or lightweight fabric the same colour as garment fabric, about $1\frac{1}{2}$in. wide and 1in. longer than buttonhole. Crease at centre, and place over buttonhole marking on right side of fabric. Pin carefully.

Using 15–20 stitches per inch, stitch $\frac{1}{8}$in. each side of crease, squaring stitching across end.

Slash end between stitching from centre to within $\frac{1}{4}$in. of each end. Clip to the four corners, forming a triangle at each end. Do not clip stitching.

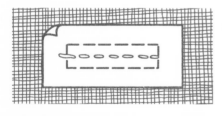

Turn organza piece through slash to wrong side. Press seam and organza piece away from opening, forming a 'window'. Make sure organza does not show from the outside. This is the size of the finished buttonhole.

Cut two straight pieces of your garment fabric each $1\frac{1}{2}$in. wide and 1in. longer than buttonhole. Press each piece in half lengthwise.

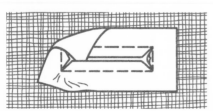

Unfold each piece and with right sides together, machine-baste them together along pressed fold. Remove this basting when garment is finished.

Re-fold each piece with wrong sides together. Press.

Place basted piece over 'window' on wrong side of garment with seam at centre. Pin at ends.

Turn garment away from buttonhole exposing seam. Using 15–20 stitches per inch, stitch over previous stitching through seam, organza and basted pieces on long edges, extending stitching to end of the piece.

Stitch each 'triangle' to organza from wide end to point. Trim excess buttonhole fabric. Press.

If you have made buttonhole before attaching interfacing to the garment, mark buttonhole on interfacing $\frac{1}{4}$in. larger than the finished buttonhole. Cut out this area. Attach interfacing to wrong side of garment; bring buttonhole through opening in interfacing. Hand-sew to interfacing.

When garment is finished, slip-stitch facing opening over buttonhole.

  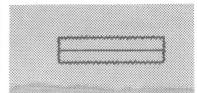

BUTTON LOOPS

Button loops are normally used to fasten over ball buttons. The loops may be made from braid or satin cording, or from bias strips of the garment fabric.

To cut bias strips of fabric, lay fabric flat and fold down one corner so that the crosswise threads of the fabric run in the same direction as the lengthwise threads. The true bias of the fabric is the diagonal edge formed by the fold, and fabric cut on this bias has the maximum amount of 'give'. Trim away the triangular corner area, then on the remaining fabric mark widths for the bias strips you require parallel with the cut diagonal edge. Cut the strips.

To join the strips together, with right sides facing, lap ends so that the strips are at right angles to each other. Stitch on the straight grain, starting and ending at point where strips cross each other. Press seam open and trim to $\frac{1}{4}$in. Trim away extending points.

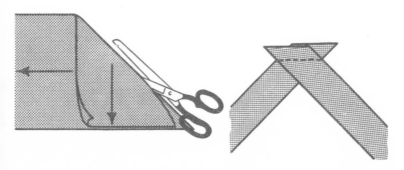

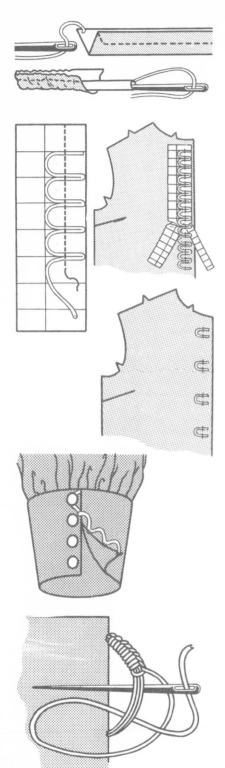

To make button loops—or rouleau loops, as they are sometimes known—cut enough true bias strips of fabric 1⅛in. wide. Fold strips in half, lengthwise, with right sides together.

Stitch ¼in. from fold, stretching bias gently while stitching. To turn bias right side out, fasten a strong thread to one end with a needle. Draw needle, eye end forward, through the fold, turning bias to right side as you work.

If your buttons are small and placed close together, use the following method to form loops:

On a piece of paper draw a line ⅝in. from one edge to represent seamline. Draw another line to the left of the first one, the width of the loop you have made. Crosswise through these lines draw lines the length of each loop. Using a continuous strip of rouleau tubing, form loops between markings, as shown in the diagram. Stitch along seamline, catching in loops as you stitch. Carefully pin loops (and paper) to garment on the right side of fabric where finished loops will be. Place stitching along seamline of garment. Have loops away from edge of garment. Stitch along seamline, and tear paper away.

If buttons are large or spaced apart, then use the following method to attach loops to garment:

Cut each loop separately. Add 1¼in. seam allowance to measurement of each loop (for a ⅝in. seam).

Baste loop to garment on right side of fabric where finished loops will be. Have loops away from edge of garment.

Loops may be also sewn to garment after it is finished. Using a continuous strip, sew on the loops along the edge where fastening is required, or slightly back from the edge on the wrong side. Use small stitches between each loop.

Thread loops

Sew several strands of thread on one edge of the opening where fastening is required. Work buttonhole or blanket stitch, close together, over the strands, using needle eye end forwards.

Chinese ball buttons

These are also made from rouleau strips of bias cut fabric, or from ready-made braid or satin cording.

Loop cord as shown in diagram. Loop again over and under first loop. Then loop a third time, weaving through other two loops. Keep loops open while working (you may find it easier to pin them to a flat surface while you work). Now ease loops together, gradually losing the slackness in the loops, and shaping into a tight, even-sized ball. Trim ends and sew them flat to the underside of buttons.

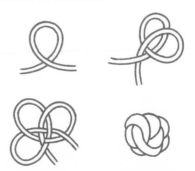

Details that count

If you have mastered all the sewing techniques so far described, you should by this time be able to make an attractive, serviceable garment. This chapter deals with the extra, professional touches you can give to your sewing: the details that make all the difference between a straightforward 'home-made' garment and a garment with a couture finish.

PRESSING

Far from being an 'extra' detail, pressing is one of the most vital and important parts of dressmaking. Correct and careful pressing will give even the simplest garment a beautiful tailored finish—it can even help to minimise small defects in the construction of a garment. Bad pressing however, or inadequate pressing can ruin the most expertly made outfit.

Never begin dressmaking until you have all your pressing equipment out—iron, ironing board, sleeve board, pressing mitt, steam dolly and pressing cloths. This is an important golden rule!

Only by pressing every seam as it is sewn, before being crossed with a second seam, can you achieve a really professional look for your garment. It is also a great deal easier to work this way than to try to do all the pressing when the garment is made up. In fact if you press as you sew there will be very little final pressing required. Remember too that there is a difference between pressing and ironing: pressing is a lifting and lowering motion; ironing is a sliding and pushing motion.

As a rule, most seams—unless instructed otherwise in your pattern—should be pressed open as soon as they are sewn. A neat trick, however, is to press all seams open first, even if subsequently they are to be pressed to one side (e.g. in collars and facings). This will give a fine seamline, will help shape the seam when needed, and will enable you to turn and press facings more easily.

Press on the inside of your garment whenever possible. When it is necessary to press on the outside, always use a pressing cloth. If you have been unlucky enough to cause a shine on the outside of your garment try removing it either by pressing on the outside of the garment over a scrap of your garment fabric, or alternatively over a piece of heavy brown paper.

Always press garments with the grain of the fabric.

Shape is often sewn into a garment with curved darts, curved seams and eased seams, so press these seams and darts with special care. Use a tailor's ham to press these areas, placing the ham underneath the seam or dart, and pressing the curved section on the ham. If you do not possess a ham, use a towel well wrapped in a piece of clean white cloth.

With fine fabrics, prevent seam impression showing through to the right side of the material by placing strips of brown paper between the seam allowance and the fabric.

Pressing collars
A perfect collar needs perfect handling in pressing. After all the necessary seam allowance is trimmed away, turn collar through and manipulate the right side of collar into the wrong side until $\frac{1}{8}$in. of the top collar appears on the under collar. Baste round to hold in position, and press carefully. If after removing basting the collar is marked, re-press it.

Pressing hems
Some Paris couture garments leave the hem unpressed, but if a pressed and sharp look is desired, hems are handled with great care and attention. The stitches of the hem should not appear on the right side nor should a sharp line indicate the extent of the allowance left as a hem. If using a heavy fabric, place a layer of fabric of the same thickness and texture as the garment fabric alongside the finished edge of the hem, and press. This helps the line not to show through on the right side. Press the edge carefully over a damp cloth, then over a dry cloth without pulling. While the steam is still trapped between the layers of the fabric, smooth over the hem with a piece of clean smooth wood. This sharpens the line of the hem. Always press a hem on the right side of the garment.

Pressing for different fabric types
Cotton and linen need a hot iron. Many cottons, especially the crease-resistant variety, benefit from steam pressing. Wool needs a medium iron. When pressing on the right side of the fabric, you must use a dry pressing cloth under the iron. If the garment needs steam pressing on the right side, a dry cloth must still be placed next to the fabric, then a damp one on top of that. Use a steam dolly for pressing seams. Silk and synthetics need a cool iron on the wrong side of the fabric.

TOP-STITCHING
Top-stitching can be used as a decorative finish, and to add an accent to the lines of a simple garment. The stitching must be straight and even. Unless you have a very accurate eye, use one of the following guides for stitching:
1. Throat plate of sewing machine with markings in eighths of an inch.
2. Seam guides that attach to bed of sewing machine.
3. Attach strip of self-adhesive tape to machine the desired distance from the needle.
4. For top-stitching not on an edge (or not in a straight line) make a row of hand-basting where the top-stitching will be, then stitch along the basted line. Do not stitch over basting. The type of thread you use for top-stitching is determined by your fabric. The regular thread with which you are sewing your garment is suitable for fine and lightweight fabrics. On heavier fabrics or for more visible top-stitching, use a slightly stronger thread, or even two or three strands of embroidery stranded cotton.

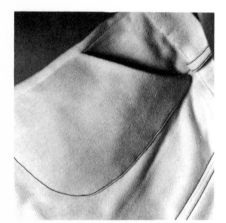

Top-stitching can be used to accent pockets and seams.

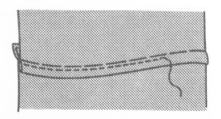

Pretty dress for a teenager has tucks under the bustline, and sleeves gathered in at wrists with elastic.

Wide tucks are equally spaced across the bodice of a little girl's dress.

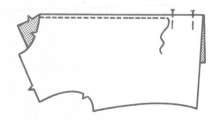

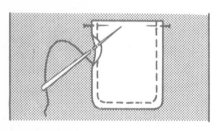

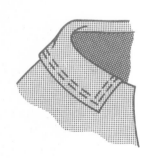

Always top-stitch on right side of fabric. Test on a scrap of fabric first of all. Where a garment is lined to the edge, top-stitching along the front, neck and sleeve edges will keep the lining from rolling to the right side.

Patch pockets can be effectively top-stitched before being attached to the garment, then slip-stitched invisibly in place to the garment.

The soft, rolled look along an edge, featured in many couturier garments, can be achieved in the following way:

Make one or two rows of top-stitching along the edge or seam. Pad the area between the edge and the stitching or between each row of stitching, using several lengths of wool yarn. Use a bodkin or heavy needle (eye end forward) to insert yarn from the end of stitching.

A simple decorative touch can be added to a collar by working two rows of top-stitching, using a longer than average stitch, and sometimes with contrasting thread instead of matching thread.

TUCKS

Tucks serve two purposes: for decoration and also for fitting. The basic types of tucks are as follows:

Pin tuck

This is a narrowly stitched tuck most often used on blouses made of a lightweight fabric such as batiste or organdie. On the right side of garment, fold along the tuck marking, and stitch as close to the fold as possible.

Wide tuck

These are similar to pin tucks but usually measure at least $\frac{1}{2}$in. across, if not wider. They are usually marked on the pattern piece with a solid line and a broken or dotted line. On the right side of garment, fold along the solid line and take to broken line. Stitch along broken line. Sometimes the tucks will be indicated by a solid line in the centre, with broken or dotted lines on each side of the centre solid line. On the right side of garment, fold along the solid line, and match the broken lines. Stitch along broken lines.

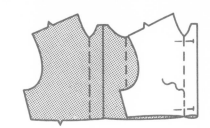

Corded tucks

Encase cord on the wrong side of the garment, then stitch tuck, using a cording or zipper foot on your machine.

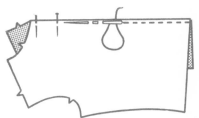

Hand-sewn tuck

Instead of machine-stitching a pin tuck (usually on fine and sheer fabrics) make small running stitches by hand close to the fold.

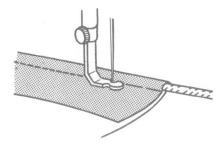

FINISHING TRICKS

Turning curved edges

If the curve to be turned is an inside one—that is, curving towards the body of the garment—clip to stay-stitching, which should have been done on seamline, before turning.

If the curve is an outside one—that is, curving away from the body of the garment—notch the curves in V-shapes to the stay-stitching before turning. This is done so the outer edge which is longer than the seamline will lie flat when the curve is turned.

Turning a facing

A professional-looking facing should be clean and flat along the edge and should stay permanently in place without rolling. To achieve this, proceed as follows:

If edge to be faced is curved or bias, stay-stitch it, and if material is loosely woven or stretchy, then stay-stitch the edge of the facing as well.

With right sides together, stitch facing to garment. Layer and clip the seam.

If the area is squared, clip into corners of the square. Press the layered seam towards the facing. On outside, under-stitch the facing to pressed seam close to seamline. Turn facing to inside and press, letting edge roll to inside so seamline does not show on right side. Catch facing to garment with a few stitches at garment seams. Alternatively catch-stitch the facing invisibly right round to the garment, as described for catch-stitch method of hem finishing (see page 33).

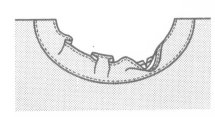

Finishing faced openings

If a garment fastens all the way to the hem in front or back, the hem or any faced opening at the bottom of the garment should be finished with a neat enclosed corner.

With facing turned to outside, stitch facing to garment on the hemline. Trim off corner at fold edge.

Trim facing edge below stitching line to about $\frac{1}{4}$in. wide. Trim garment edge just slightly wider, trimming from fold edge to within $\frac{3}{4}$in. of inner edge of facing.

Press trimmed seam open. Then turn facing to inside and press. Turn and press remainder of hem and finish by method chosen.

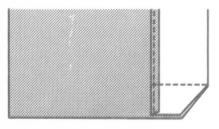

TO MITRE CORNERS

Turn seam allowance under and press.

Open out pressed seam allowance and turn corner under on a diagonal line running through point where the first two pressed lines meet. Press to make a third crease.

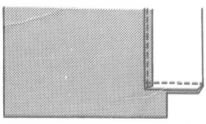

Trim off corner about $\frac{1}{8}$in. from pressed diagonal crease. Fold trimmed corner to wrong side on the diagonal crease. Fold remainder of piece on pressed seam allowances.

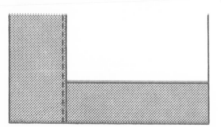

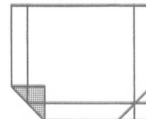

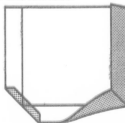

Linings
and interfacings

LININGS

It is essential that most heavyweight garments, such as coats, suits, and some skirts, are lined. This will prolong the life of the garment, and give it a much better 'hang'. A lining in fact gives a beautiful, professional finish to the inside of a fashion garment and may be used in addition to an underlining (see below). Constructed as a separate unit, a lining is made by following the same sewing steps as for the garment, omitting collars, cuffs, facings, zippers and so on. A lining protects a garment from shape changes during wear and helps reduce wrinkling. A seam finish is seldom required for the garment (unless the fabric is inclined to fray easily) because the wrong side of the lining is placed against the wrong side of the garment, thereby concealing all seam allowances.

If you do not want a full lining for a garment, but you do need to give the fabric support or strength, then you should use an underlining. This differs from a full lining in that the pieces are cut from the same pattern pieces as the garment and joined to the outer fabric pieces before seams are stitched; thus the two layers are handled as one during construction.

Both lining and underlining fabrics should be chosen with care to complement the garment fabric. For lightweight fabrics, choose a lightweight crêpe or silk-like rayon lining; for medium-weight fabrics, taffeta, silk surah or polished cotton; heavyweight fabrics should have heavy taffeta, satin, or rayon twill.

First, a few general hints on lining a garment:
1. Machine-stitch along seam allowance on front and neck edges of lining, then press these edges (clipping curves first) to the wrong side along this stitching. Make sure stitching does not show on the right side.
2. A row of machine-stitching along seam allowance of front and back facings of the garment before stitching them to the garment will help when lapping and stitching the lining to the facing.
3. Do not slip-stitch the facing exactly at the lower edge, but instead loosely hand-sew facing to hem about $\frac{1}{4}$in. from lower edge, then turn under and hand-sew raw edge of facing to the hem.
4. If you do not have a dress form, place garment wrong side out on a hanger when pinning the lining to it. The lining should be finished about $\frac{3}{4}$ or 1in. above the hem of the garment.
5. Hand-sew the lining sleeves to the armhole of the garment for an extra couturier touch.
6. When slip-stitching lining over hem at lower end of sleeve, baste lining to garment about $\frac{1}{2}$ to $\frac{3}{4}$in. above lower edge of lining. Then turn the lining back and slip-stitch lining to hem about $\frac{1}{4}$in. from lower edge of lining.

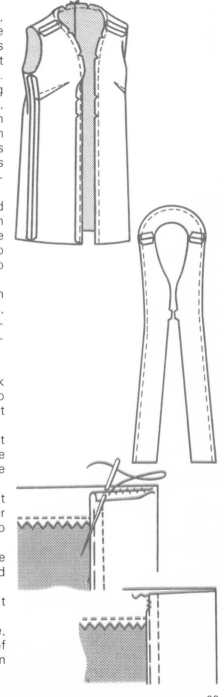

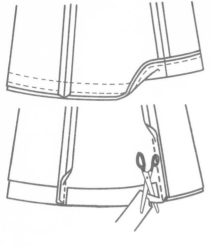

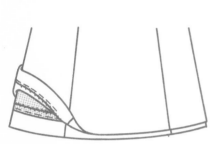

Lining a dress
Method 1. Working lining and dress pieces together as one. Cut lining as dress pieces, except facings and collar. Baste lining and dress fabric pieces together $\frac{1}{2}$in. from the raw edges and through centre lines of darts. Make up dress in usual way. Then mark your hem length an even distance from the floor. Press up hem and trim to an even width.

Unfold hem and hand-baste lining to dress about $\frac{1}{2}$in. below hem fold with long and short running stitches. Finish hem by chosen method.

Alternatively, trim hem portion of lining away along fold line, then finish hem by chosen method.

Method 2. Working lining and dress as separate units. Cut lining same as dress, except facings and collar. First make up dress, leaving neckline and armhole unfinished.

Then make the lining leaving the opening for the zipper 1in. longer than in the dress.

With wrong sides together, pin lining to dress at neckline and armhole edges.

Match darts, seams, centres and notches. Have raw edges even. Turn under edges of lining and slip-stitch along stitching on tape of zipper.

Machine-baste neck and armhole edges together $\frac{1}{2}$in. from edge. Finish neck edge.

For dress with a sleeve, attach sleeve to dress. Then sew sleeve lining and pin to sleeve wrong sides together, matching markings. Turn under seam allowance on lining and hand-sew over armhole seam. Trim sleeve lining even with lower edge of sleeve. Turn under $\frac{1}{2}$in. on sleeve lining and slip-stitch over sleeve hem.

For a sleeveless dress attach armhole facing. Make dress hem first. Then make the lining hem so that it is $\frac{1}{2}$in. shorter than dress.

Lining a skirt
Method 1. Working lining and skirt pieces together as one. Cut lining same as skirt pieces (except waistband). Mark notches and centres on skirt. Mark darts, notches and centres on linings.

With marked side up, pin lining to wrong side of skirt pieces, raw edges even. Match notches and centres. Baste together $\frac{1}{2}$in. from raw edges and through centre line of darts.

Make up skirt in usual way. Mark your hem length an even distance from the floor, press up hem and trim to an even width.

Unfold hem and hand-baste lining to skirt about $\frac{1}{2}$in. below hem fold with long and short running stitches. Finish hem by chosen method.

Alternatively trim hem portion of lining away along fold line, then finish hem by chosen method.

Method 2. Working lining and skirt as separate units. Cut lining same as skirt pieces (except waistband).

First make up skirt, except waistband and hem.

Make the lining, leaving the opening for the zipper 1in. longer than in the skirt. Press seams open and darts away from centre. With wrong sides together, pin lining to skirt. Match darts, seams, centres and notches. Have raw edges together at the

Shift dress, summer and winter versions—making instructions are on page 154.

Child's quilted anorak has a front zip fastening, and a hood with draw-string cord—making instructions on page 120.

waistline. Turn under left edges of lining and slip-stitch along stitching on tape of zipper.

Machine-baste waistline edges together $\frac{1}{2}$in. from edge. Sew waistband to skirt.

Make the skirt hem first, then make the lining hem so that it is $\frac{1}{2}$in. shorter than skirt.

Lining a jacket

Make up jacket and lining separately. In lining make a $\frac{1}{2}$-in. pleat down centre back; press in place. With wrong sides together, put lining into jacket. Loosely stitch side seams together as far as jacket hem.

Now carefully pin lining to jacket round armholes, matching shoulder seams, and easing to fit as necessary. Stitch—again fairly loosely—round armhole seams.

Turn in raw edges of lining round neck and front edges along seam allowance. Carefully pin in place to jacket front and neck facing. Insert pins at right angles to lining. Do not pull lining too tightly. Turn up lower hem of lining to about $\frac{1}{2}$in. above lower edge of jacket. Slip-stitch lining to jacket round front and neck edges.

Slip-stitch lining hem invisibly to jacket hem by working underneath lining. Turn in sleeve lining hems and slip-stitch to jacket sleeve hems in a similar way. Press garment carefully.

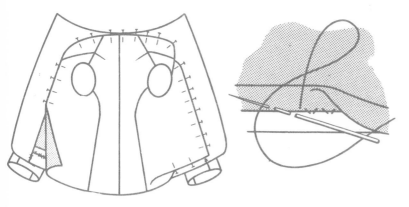

Pretty quick—lining tips

Try sewing the lining to your garment before the facing and hem, and then finish both hem and facing with a narrow bias binding cut from lining fabric. This is a real couture touch.

Alternatively, trim edge where lining and facing meet with a decorative ribbon or braid. Or use a ric-rac braid inserted in the seam so that only half of the ric-rac braid shows when the lining is in place.

For a really elegant touch, stitch vertical rows of flat lace on to right side of lining fabric before stitching lining in place. Before sewing in lining sleeves cut another front and back lining section of chiffon or a sheer fabric and place it over right side of lace-trimmed section. Then sew ready-gathered lace edging into the seam where the lining and facing meet.

An attractive 'ensemble' look can be achieved by making a suit blouse and the jacket lining to match. Make a matching scarf as well to complete the total look!

INTERFACINGS

Interfacing is the material inserted between the garment's fabric and its lining or its facing to add crispness, or for permanent shaping of areas such as collars, cuffs, lapels and so on. When used under buttons and buttonholes, it also strengthens those areas which have to withstand extra strain.

Interfacing materials may be made especially for interfacing purposes, or they may be a fabric which is also used for making garments, such as cotton broadcloth, organdie or taffeta.

The materials made especially for interfacing are of two general types: woven and non-woven. Within these two general types are many variations in weight, texture and colour.

Woven interfacings

These are made in a similar way to woven fabrics with lengthwise and crosswise threads, and must therefore be cut on the grain, as you do any other woven fabric. This woven group of materials includes the various weights and types of canvas.

Non-woven interfacings

These are the most widely used interfacings. They are a combination of natural and man-made fibres joined together by binder systems to give a non-woven fabric without lengthwise or crosswise threads. The interfacing may be cut in any direction and it cannot fray; it is usually washable and dry-cleanable and guarantees permanent shape to the garment in which it is applied. Available in heavy, medium, lightweight or sheer fabrics, usually sold in 32 or 36in. widths, and in a choice of black or white. If you are in doubt about which weight of interfacing to choose, always use the lighter one.

Iron-on interfacing

Certain weights of non-woven interfacing are available with an iron-on finish—you simply apply the interfacing to the wrong side of fabric, with the powdered (rough) side of the interfacing against wrong side of fabric, and press with a hot, preferably steam, iron. Press evenly all over, and leave for a few minutes. The temperature of your iron will be determined by the type of fabric you are using for your garment.

Where to use interfacing

Generally interfacing should be used to give body and shape to a garment and to improve its finished appearance. It should be used in all collars, cuffs, facings, behind buttonholes, pockets or for any edges that must remain firm. A lightweight grade of interfacing can be used to give a permanent knife edge appearance to skirt pleats—cut interfacing to the length of the knife pleat, less hem, and machine to the pleat backing; secure with the hem. When closing darts, stitch interfacing as one with the fabric, ensuring that the darts are not run off too abruptly. Taper off over the last inch. Complete underskirts of interfacing can be used for evening dresses and most flared styles of skirts and dresses.

When interfacing a collar or pocket flap, the interfacing should be cut $\frac{1}{16}$in. smaller than the actual pattern to ensure the flap or collar will roll and lay flat when turned; after cutting out interfacing section, trim outer corners of interfacing diagonally where seamlines meet.

Always layer seams with interfacing—trim interfacing close to the stitching, trim one seam allowance to $\frac{1}{4}$in., the other to $\frac{3}{8}$in. Trim outer corners diagonally.

If interfacing has a dart, cut through the centre of the dart, lap cut edges, matching dart lines. Stitch zig-zag stitching at the point and trim lapped edges.

In lined garments, to avoid ridges when the garment is pressed, extend the interfacing beyond facings or hems. In unlined garments, the facing should always extend beyond interfacing.

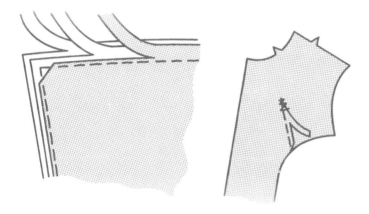

To interface a neckline

Method 1. Machine-baste interfacing to wrong side of front and back of garment before stitching the shoulder seam. In this way the interfacing is sandwiched between the garment fabric and seam allowances, and so provides a protection against pressing marks. Stitch shoulder seams, and attach facing in the normal way.

Method 2. This is a neat finish to use for fabrics which are inclined to fray. Stitch shoulder seams of front and back neck facing. Then stitch shoulder seams of front and back neck interfacing. Press all seams open. With right sides together, pin facing and interfacing together along unnotched edge. Stitch $\frac{1}{4}$in. from edge.

Press seam open. Turn right side out and press. Attach to garment in usual way.

Method 3. When a neckline construction includes gathers or intricate seaming the interfacing will have to be attached to the facing. Pin interfacing to wrong side of front and back neck facing. Trim outside corners of back interfacing diagonally. Machine-baste interfacing $\frac{1}{2}$in. from raw edges. Trim interfacing close to stitching. Then stitch neck facings together at shoulder seams. Press seams open. Stitch under $\frac{1}{4}$in. on unnotched edge. Attach facing to garment in usual way.

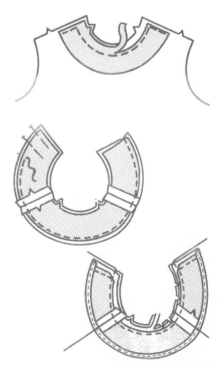

Finishing touches

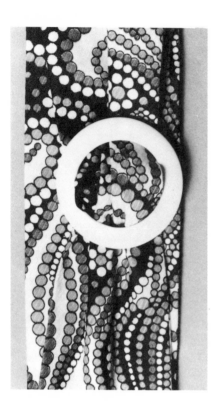

A finishing touch by way of trimming or accessory is a very personal matter: the right choice of finishing detail can give an outfit the hallmark of your personality. It can also do a lot to lift an otherwise plain and rather anonymous dress into couture class; and it can give an up-to-the-minute 'this year' look to a dress from last season, for fashions in trimmings and accessories, if anything, change even more than the dress styles themselves.

BELTS
Perhaps the simplest trimming of all, yet one which can totally alter the look of a dress or other outfit. It is a good idea to build up a wardrobe of belt types and colours—they are quick and easy to make, and a good way to use up fabric remnants.

Flat tie belt
Method 1 (quick and easy). Cut a long straight strip of fabric, $3\frac{1}{2}$in. by 54in. This will comfortably fit an average size waist 24–26in. For a size larger add 2in. to the length; for a size smaller, cut length 2in. less. Turn in $\frac{1}{2}$in. at each short end and press, then turn in and press 1in. down one long edge, $\frac{1}{2}$in. down the other. Fold the belt in half lengthways, wrong sides together, so the long edges meet exactly. Pin, then machine down this seam as close to the edges as possible. Machine across short ends, also as close to the edges as possible. Remove pins, and press well.

Method 2 (couture method). Cut a long straight strip of fabric, 3in. by 54in. Follow instructions in method 1 for fitting to your waist size. Fold strip in half lengthways, right sides together, and machine long edges together, leaving a gap of about 3–4in. unstitched in the centre. Stitch 1in. from edge of fabric. Press the seam open, making sure it lies along centre of belt, and stitch across the short ends, $\frac{1}{2}$in. from edge of fabric. Layer the turnings and clip corners.

Turn the belt right side out by pushing the ends through the gap in stitching with the help of the knob end of a knitting needle. Close the gap in the seams with neat slip stitches, then give the belt a final press.

Rouleau belt
A rouleau belt is made from bias-cut strips of fabric (see page 61). The following directions will make a belt about $\frac{1}{2}$in. wide, but you can make rouleaux any width you like. In general the strip of fabric should be four times wider than the finished width you require—e.g. for a $\frac{1}{2}$in. wide belt, you would have to cut a strip of fabric 2in. wide. The turnings for this type of belt are not trimmed, but left inside the rouleau to pad it and give it its characteristic roundness.

Button-up skirt has its plaid pattern carefully matched across the centre front opening.

Cut and join sufficient bias strips of fabric to make one long strip about 54in. Press open the short joining seams. Fold strip in half lengthways right sides together, and stitch long edge together ½in. from fabric edge. When seam is stitched, cut a tiny notch out of the folded edge (not the seam allowance) about 1in. from one end. Insert a hair grip into the rouleau, lower part of grip into end of fold, the upper part into the notched hole. Now move the hair grip along the length of the rouleau and it should emerge at the other end, pulling the rouleau through to the right side.

To finish, tuck in the raw edges at ends of rouleau and over-sew with tiny stitches or, for a quick finish, leave raw ends and tie each into a single knot. Pull knot tightly and trim off the ends close to the knot.

Alternative method. Fold bias strip in half lengthways, right sides together, over a length of fine but strong string, making sure the string extends for a good 3in. beyond the rouleau at each end. Machine across one end to hold the string in position, and trim off string close to stitching. Stitch down the long edges, ½in. from edge of fabric. At the unstitched end, pull gently on the string and the rouleau should be pulled through to the right side. Snip off the string close to the stitching.

Finish belt as for first method.

Leather belt

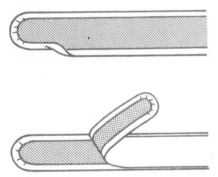

Cut leather to give length, width and shape of belt required, adding on ⅜in. to all edges for seam allowances. Cut a strip of lining fabric to exactly the same size. Cut a strip of interfacing to the finished size of belt required (i.e. without the ⅜in. seam allowance).

Glue interfacing to wrong side of leather using fabric glue. Make ¼in. clips on curved edges of leather.

Turn belt seam allowance over interfacing and glue lightly in place, or if preferred hold with catch stitches to interfacing.

Press lining seam allowance under ½in. Place lining over belt, wrong sides together, and hand-sew neatly in position. Stitch one end of belt over the bar of a suitable buckle or finish with press studs, or metal belt clasps.

Plaited belt

Buy three narrow leather belts in three different colours or all in the same colour, whichever you prefer. Plait the three belts together, starting and ending plait about 6in. from each end. Neatly stitch the three ends together on wrong side at start and at end of plait to prevent the plait coming undone.

Crochet belt

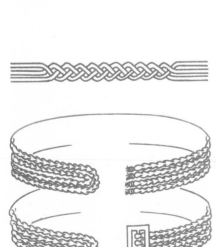

Work several lengths of simple chain stitch crochet in fairly thick wool, each length to measure twice your waist size plus 12in. Place all the finished lengths together, double them (so one loop is inside the other) then form into belt shape (see diagram, left). Hand-sew rows of chains together securely on underside. Stitch across straight end, then sew this end over bar of buckle.

If wished the finished belt can be mounted on belt backing or petersham to give it more stability.

Cummerbund

Cut soft fabric 9 or 10in. wide, the measurement of your waist size plus seam allowances and an overlap. Mark at centre point of measurements, and at this marking and at the ends make three rows of gathers to desired width, and stitch boning over gathers at front edge and right-hand side. Turn and hem long sides; face front end. Bind back end on inside. Lap front end over back. Fasten with hooks and eyes.

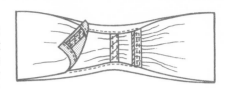

Belt carriers

Chain loop. Working with a long double thread, take two small horizontal stitches just above the belt position on dress to secure. Take another stitch but do not pull stitch closed—leave a loop wide enough to put thumb and forefinger through. Place thumb and forefinger through this loop, and pull a second loop of thread through. Still holding on to the second loop, pull first loop tight. Now pull a third loop through the second in the same way. Continue in this way, always holding on to a loop as you pull the previous one tight, and leaving needle dangling at the end of the thread. When your chain is long enough, slip needle through last loop and draw up tight. Fasten off with a few small stitches at base of belt position.

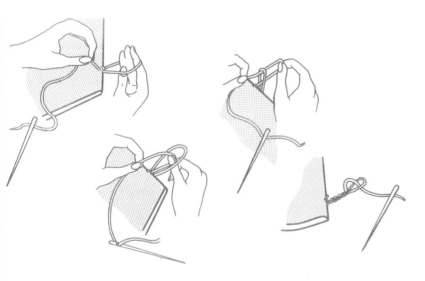

Buttonhole loop. Again, use a double thread. Begin by making a 'core' by passing needle through the fabric above and below the belt position two or three times, so you have several long 'stitches' across area of the required belt loop. Now, working from top of 'core' down, work buttonhole stitches all the way down in this way: work from right to left, taking needle behind 'core' and inserting point of needle through loop of thread. Pull stitch closed, but not too tight. Continue in this way until entire 'core' is closely covered with buttonhole stitches. Fasten off thread.

Rouleau loop. Make a rouleau strip of fabric (see page 76), using only a small bias strip of fabric. Stitch top and bottom of strip in position to right side of dress.

BRAIDS AND RIBBONS

Many of the attractive embroidered and novelty ribbon trimmings sold by the yard in haberdashery stores are tightly woven
so cannot be shaped around curves easily. Use them therefore to
trim straight edges, such as the front openings of jackets and
blouses. Corners can be mitred to make a neat square or point.

Ribbon trimming may be applied with a row of top-stitching
(see page 64) on each edge, or alternatively the trimming may
be hand-sewn in place with invisible stitches.

Braid trimmings, available in a wide range of colours, types
and widths, can usually be shaped with a warm iron. Stretch the
outer curve and shrink or ease the inner curve until the braid is
the shape you want. Since there is no right or wrong side on
flat woven braid, it may be reversed when applying it.

Flat woven braid may be applied with top-stitching on each
edge, but novelty braids should be hand-sewn with invisible
stitches. Jewelled braids are often available for trimming party
clothes—usually these are backed with a loose knit or braid
strip to give the trimming flexibility. They can be used on curves
as well as straight edges. When pinning trimming to garment,
gently stretch outer curve and ease inner curve.

Never try to machine-stitch jewelled trimmings—always sew
on carefully by hand.

Deliciously soft, floating feather trimming is sometimes
available, sold by the yard. This may be hand-sewn to your
garment, or held in place with thread carriers of matching thread
so that the trimming may be easily removed when the dress
needs cleaning.

FRINGES

Ready-made fringing in an assortment of colours, materials and
widths can be bought from most haberdashery stores and
departments. Sometimes the fringing has a novelty braid-like
edge which is most effective sewn on top of an edge. Other
fringing has a flat edge, and should be stitched into a seam.

Two easy-to-apply trimmings: ric-rac braid for a sundress (left) and lace edging for the sleeve of a baby's angel top.

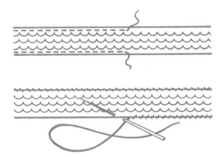

The same basic dress transformed with different trimmings.

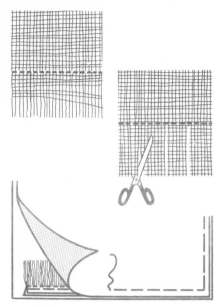

A self-fringe is the easiest kind of fringe to make on a coarse weave fabric. Before fringing trim the fabric edge on the grain. Measure in from the edge the desired length of the fringe and pull a thread. Just above this pulled thread, make a line of machine stitching. Then pull the next thread below the first one pulled and continue pulling threads to the edge. Starting in this way at the top of the fringe and working down prevents the threads from tangling.

On closely-woven fabrics, if you cut the fabric up to the stitching at intervals, it will be easier to pull out the crosswise threads.

A separate fringe can also be made of self fabric and then stitched into a seam. Cut fabric the width you want your fringe to be, plus ⅝in. seam allowance. Stitch ⅝in. from one long edge, then pull out threads to the stitching as for self-fringe described above.

On lighter weight fabrics, such as silks and satins, several layers made of this type of fringe will give a rich luxury look to a garment. Baste several of these layers together, with raw edges even, and then sew into a seam.

To make a knotted fringe, narrowly hem the edge to which the fringe will be attached. Thread a large-eyed darning needle with two or more strands of fringing yarn. Turn under the edge to which the fringe is to be attached. Working from right to left, bring needle up through turned edge of fabric. Take stitches about ¼in. apart, leaving loops of the desired length between stitches. When a sufficient number of loops have been made, cut them and knot the yarn of each stitch. Trim lower ends evenly.

Alternatively individual lengths of yarn can be cut to slightly more than double the depth of fringe required. Two or more strands are then placed together, doubled, and the looped end pulled through edge of fabric where fringe is required, using a crochet hook to catch hold of strands. Pull the cut ends of strands through doubled loop to fasten.

COVERED PRESS STUDS

To cover press studs, cut two circles of lining fabric twice the size of the press stud. Make small running stitches by hand along the edge of each circle. Do not fasten or break the thread. Place press stud sections face down over the circle. Pull up thread tightly on each circle and secure with several stitches. Sew to garment.

Your needle will find the little sewing holes in the press stud quite easily—fastening and unfastening the stud several times will bring the knob of the stud through the fabric.

COVERED HOOKS AND EYES

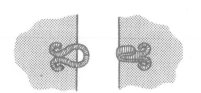

To cover hooks and eyes, sew hook and eye to the garment with blanket stitches, and then continue covering remaining portion of hook and eye with blanket stitches. Work in the following way: bring needle through to right side of fabric. Hold thread down, forming a loop. Insert needle over hook and out through loop. Pull thread loop forming a stitch. Continue in this way until the hook is completely covered. Be careful to keep the stitches close together.

EMBROIDERY

Machine-worked embroidery. Many modern sewing machines are capable of producing a wide range of attractive decorative embroidery stitching. An automatic zigzag machine, for instance, will produce decorative patterns automatically, which means the work can be carried out both quickly and easily. Some of these models have built-in discs and one or two selectors which may be set for any stitch pattern you want. Others have an assortment of discs—you insert one for each stitch pattern. Some machines even provide both types and hundreds of beautiful patterns may be formed by combining the drop-in and built-in discs.

The decision to use decorative zigzag embroidery should be made when the garment you are making is still at the planning stage. Often the stitching will extend through a seam allowance and must therefore be applied before the seam is stitched. Alternatively, the decorative stitching may be confined to a small section of the garment, then it is easier to handle this section alone under the needle than on the completed garment.

Lurex, mercerised or silk sewing threads are ideal for decorative stitching. They may blend with the fabric or be a contrast

Examples of embroidery worked on a modern sewing machine. Far left: concentric circles of decorative stitching. Top: decorative stitch patterns worked in brightly-coloured threads. Below: bands of decorative stitching in gold and silver Lurex at the neckline and cuffs of a silk evening dress.

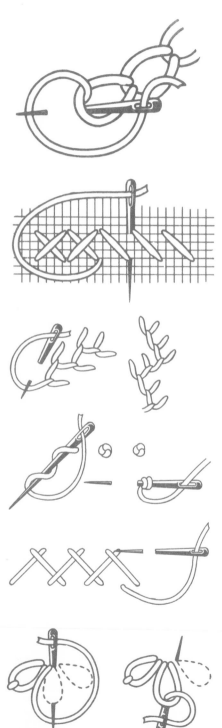

in colour and texture. For an unusual effect, try embroidering with variegated colour thread—it gradually changes colour and looks particularly attractive when used for flower-like designs.

You can do decorative zigzag embroidery on almost any fabric: on soft fabrics use a backing of crisp lawn, organdie, organza or fine tulle. On other types of fabrics you will achieve the best results with lightweight interfacings, particularly the iron-on variety. Always make a test before working on your garment. Use a scrap of the same material and adjust machine for tension and stitch width. When the work is completed, the backing can be cut away close to the stitching with small, sharp scissors.

Border designs of unlimited variety can be created by combining several stitch patterns. Use a border design as you would a braid, around the hem, through the bodice and sleeve section, in a yoke, and on collars, cuffs, belts and pockets.

Refer to your machine instruction manual to find out exactly what decorative stitching your machine is capable of. As soon as you become familiar with your machine and all its capabilities you can then go on to create your own embroidery designs.

Hand-worked embroidery

The addition of hand-worked embroidery to a simple dress or blouse can give the garment a distinctive finishing touch. Sometimes it is possible to combine effectively machine and hand-worked embroidery. A few basic hand-embroidery stitches are given below.

Chain stitch. Work from right to left. Take a stitch along line of work; loop thread under needle point. Repeat, inserting point of needle inside first loop close to where thread came out.

Cross stitch. Work from left to right, keeping needle straight between two lines, making half the cross. To make the second half of the cross, work from right to left. For double cross stitch, make a second cross over the first, making the stitches straight, where the previous ones were diagonal.

Feather stitch. Make a blanket stitch slanted to the right. Throw thread to the left under needle and make blanket stitch slanted to the left. Repeat. For fancy feather stitch, make several blanket stitches on each side.

French knots. Mark dots where knots are to be. Bring needle out on a dot. Wind thread over needle two or three times, holding thread taut with other hand. Put needle in close to where it came out and pull up knot.

Herringbone stitch. This is similar to cross stitch (see above). Draw evenly-spaced lines and work from left to right between them. Bring needle out at lower left; take a back stitch on upper line a little to the right. Keep thread below needle. Take back stitch on lower line a little to the right; keep thread above needle. Repeat. Stitches may be worked close together for a filled effect.

Lazy daisy stitch. Bring needle out at inner point of petal. Put it in again at same place. Take a stitch towards you with thread looped under needle. Hold loop with small stitch and bring needle out at centre for next petal.

Special treatment for special clothes

TROUSERS

One of the most striking fashion developments of recent years has been the conversion of trousers from a strictly sportswear garment to a fashion item which can be worn at any hour of the day or night and in most places.

The straightforward trousers teamed with blouse or sweater is still popular but today the real secret of the success of trousers is the way it is teamed with other fashion garments: trousers with matching jackets, waistcoats or tabards; trousers with tunics or ponchos; trousers and top in a one-piece cat-suit or jumpsuit; in fact trousers with everything! And what is more — trousers in every conceivable fabric: linen, lace, Tricel, silk, wool, crêpe, brocade, cotton . . .

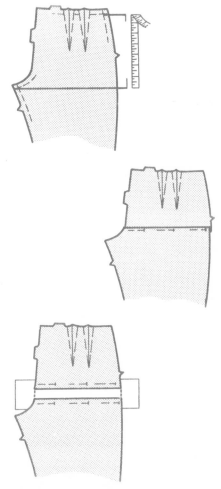

Despite what you might think, trousers are not difficult to make yourself, provided a little extra time and care are spent in making a personalised trouser shape guide. Once you have prepared this guide and provided your figure does not change too dramatically, you can adjust any paper pattern to a perfect fit.

First take and note down your measurements as follows: waist; hips at fullest point; length of outside leg from waist to ankle; crutch, measuring as explained on page 15.

Buy the pattern according to your waist measurement. If your hips are larger than the hip measurement for your size, buy the pattern according to your hip measurement. You can always make the waist smaller by stitching deeper darts and side seams. Now check your measurements against those of the pattern.

At side seam on the back pattern measure up from the depth-of-crutch line to the waistline seamline. If this measurement is the same as your crutch measurement, including the $\frac{3}{4}$in. for ease, then the crutch should fit and needs no alteration. If it is more than your measurement including the $\frac{3}{4}$in., the crutch will have to be shortened.

To do this measure up from the adjustment line marked on your pattern the amount to be shortened. Draw line across pattern. Fold pattern on the adjustment line and bring fold up to drawn line and pin. Make a similar adjustment on the pattern front.

If the measurement is less than yours including the $\frac{3}{4}$in., the crutch will have to be lengthened.

Cut apart pattern on the adjustment line, place tissue paper underneath spreading pattern the necessary length apart. Pin to paper. Make a similar adjustment to pattern front.

Measure round the upper part of your thigh, and add about $2\frac{1}{2}$in. for ease. Measure front and back pattern from seamline to seamline at same distance below the crutch at which you measured your thigh. If this measurement is less than your own, including the $2\frac{1}{2}$in., the pattern should be widened. If the

measurement is more, including the $2\frac{1}{2}$in., the pattern should be made narrower. Divide any difference by four and widen or narrow each side seam and inner leg seam by this difference.

If the outer leg length of your pattern requires adjustment, make the alterations in two places: directly above and below the knee. If the waist or hip areas of your pattern call for any alteration divide the difference between the two side seams, making sure that you divide the total amount by four. Then add or subtract the required amount as necessary graduating to nothing at the knee.

It is an excellent idea to make up a toile for your trouser fitting (see page 45) and then this fitted and perfectly adjusted shape can be superimposed on trouser patterns of various designs to ensure you achieve tailor-made trousers every time.

A few hints to help

When stitching seams, especially the crutch seam, gently stretch the fabric as it passes under your machine foot, or use your machine's special stretch stitch (if it has one) to prevent the stitching from breaking with active body movement.

Sew your seams in the same order as a tailor does—leg seams first, and then after a thorough press, the crutch seam. Remember to make your waistband loose enough so that it will be comfortable when you are sitting down, as well as standing. Be sure to follow your pattern instructions on easing the waistline of the trousers into the waistband.

Hems are particularly vulnerable on trousers. To strengthen them, sew hem binding to the raw edges; then using a blind-hem stitch on your machine, fasten them into place.

To strengthen and neaten the crutch seam, sew a small diamond of fine cotton over the meeting point of the four seams.

CHILDREN'S CLOTHES

Fashion is important to children from a very early age. Little boys and girls know when they are dressed smartly and when their clothes fit well, so if their mothers can sew and have a flair for fashion too, they are especially lucky! As a general rule, when making clothes for children, the simpler the design, the better. Choose basic styles that are quick to make, easy to fit and simple to alter as the child grows—e.g. a style which is easy to lengthen and to let out. You can always add interest by using a pretty patterned fabric or trimming the garment with decorative stitches, or a braid or ribbon edging.

Select the pattern size by a combination of chest and length measurement—never by age. The size indicated on a commercial paper. pattern will give the approximate age for which the pattern was designed, but children of the same age differ widely in height, weight and in shape. By using the chest measurement as the main guide you will have to make very few—if any— adjustments in the pattern for a good fit. Always measure the pattern and make any necessary adjustments before cutting out.

There is no economy in the use of poor-quality fabrics for children's clothes. They have a short life, and do not lend themselves to good styling, good fit or hard wear. So always buy the best you can afford, selecting fabrics that will withstand the wear and constant washing necessary for children's garments.

Trousers for him and her, in bold bright checks.

Clothes for children are usually quick and easy to make. Casual shirts, shown here, have lace-up fastening, the bell-bottomed trousers are the same basic pattern, with variations in pocket types.

Fabrics most suitable include woven checks, lawn, organdie, gaberdine, seersucker, lightweight washable wools, flannel, tweed, needlecord, towelling and jersey. Look out too for the easy-care fabrics specially designed for children's wear in synthetic blends such as Acrilan, Crimplene, Courtelle and Terylene and other mixtures and, if possible, those that need little or no ironing.

Choose colours and prints that are flattering for the hair and skin colouring of the child, and are also practical for the outfit you are making. Bold, clear colours are best for everyday wear—save the pale and pretty pastels for parties and special occasions.

Never make children's clothes too large, thinking they can be worn for a longer time. Both fit and fashion are lost along the way and often the garment is worn out and discarded long before the child grows to fit it.

Casual fashions for a teenager: safari jacket (left) and tunic and trousers (below) can be worn separately or as a complete matching ensemble. Making instructions are on pages 131 and 135.

Skirts may be made with deep hems so that they can be lengthened at any time. Allow 3 or 4in. for hems on full-gathered skirts, and about 2in. for shaped hems on flared skirts.

Tucks are a neat and practical way to allow for growth (see page 66), and may be placed in the following positions:
1. Through the hem so that the tuck is not visible on the right side.
2. On the right side just above the hem as a decorative finish, especially on lightweight fabrics.

A chain stitch is often used in preference to a regular straight machine stitch on children's clothes, as this makes letting out a simple task: just unlock the last loop of the chain formed on the underside of the tuck and pull out the stitching.

WAISTBANDS ON SKIRTS AND TROUSERS

If your weight is inclined to fluctuate so that one day your waistband fits comfortably, the next it strangles you, then fit elasticised waistbands to your skirts and trousers—and the waistband will adjust itself to whatever size your waist chooses to be!

First fold waistband pattern in half lengthwise. Then cut the waistband of your garment fabric, adding $\frac{1}{2}$in. at the fold edge. Before removing pattern, mark along lengthwise fold with chalk or long basting stitches. Transfer waistband markings to fabric.

The elastic should be the same width as the finished waistband. Cut elastic 1in. shorter than the length of your waistband. Lap elastic over right side of waistband $\frac{1}{8}$in. from marking. Pin to band with ends even. Stitch close to edge of elastic, gently stretching the elastic to fit the waistband. Now attach the waistband to skirt or trousers. Trim seam; clip curve. Press waistband out, away from the garment. Press seam towards waistband.

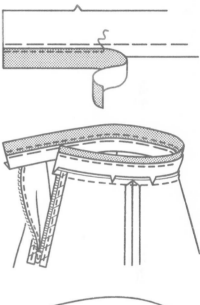

Turn in $\frac{5}{8}$in. on ends of waistband and elastic. Trim to $\frac{3}{8}$in. Turn elastic to wrong side along marking on waistband. Pin elastic over seam, stretching to fit.

Slip-stitch ends over seam, using a synthetic thread. Fasten ends with hooks and eyes.

PLEATS

Pleats are easy to cope with if you follow the carefully marked instructions on your pattern. The pattern generally indicates with arrows the direction in which the pleats are to lap. The fold (or crease) line is usually indicated by a solid line. The line to which the fold is lapped is indicated by a broken or dotted line. To avoid confusion, mark the lines with basting stitches, using a different colour thread for the two different lines.

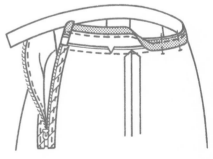

If pleats are to be pressed the lines extend the full length of the pattern. If pleats are unpressed (or soft) the lines extend from the upper edge of pattern for about 2 to 4in. If when lapping the fold to the broken line, you keep the upper edges even, your pleats will hang correctly.

It is a good idea to baste the pleats in place along the folds. But remove basting before final pressing.

On a straight skirt, it is easier to make the hem first and then to make the pleats. On a shaped skirt, make the hem after you

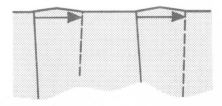

Classic cardigan suit, with co-ordinated blouse, is smart and slimming for a larger size—making instructions on page 163.

have made the pleats but before the final pressing.

The following pleats are reasonably easy to handle by the home dressmaker:
1. Straight or knife pleats. All lapping in the same direction, usually right over left.
2. Box pleat. Two straight pleats turned away from each other, forming a panel.
3. Inverted pleat. Two straight pleats turned towards each other.

Note. To help hold your pleats in place through washing or dry cleaning, and to make them easier to press, stitch close to the fold of the pleat on the wrong side of your garment, either just the length of the hem or the entire length of pleat. This can be done by hand or by machine.

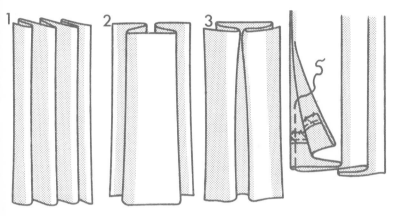

GATHERS

Gathers add softness and fullness to summer skirts and dresses. On most fabrics, the gathers can be done by machine. Use a longer than average machine stitch (the heavier the fabric, the longer the stitch).

Make a row of machine stitching on seamline, leaving a loose thread at each end. Make another row about $\frac{1}{4}$ in. from the first row within the seam allowance. You may add another row $\frac{1}{8}$ in. or $\frac{1}{4}$ in. from the first row outside the seam allowance to help control the gathers. But this row of stitching will show when the garment is finished, so only use it if you feel it is absolutely necessary.

When pinning the gathered area in a seam, match all the markings very carefully. These markings guide the position of your gathers.

Holding on to the thread ends at each end of rows of stitching, gently ease fabric over machine stitching until gathered area fits the ungathered area. Fasten thread ends around a pin in a figure of eight shape.

With a pin, bring top thread of gathers to the wrong side and knot threads to hold gathers. Again with a pin, adjust fullness evenly.

Always stitch with gathered area towards you so that you can guide gathers without puckering. Do not press gathers flat, but gently guide iron between the folds.

On full skirts, it is sometimes preferable to divide the total area to be gathered into quarters, and to gather each quarter individually.

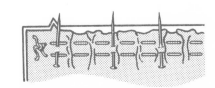

Summer suit has a swinging, knife-pleated skirt.

MAKING LINGERIE

More and more of today's young dressmakers are making their own colour co-ordinated lingerie wardrobe, complete with bras and pants. The constantly increasing range of beautiful fine synthetic fabrics suitable for underwear is difficult to resist!

The tricots are probably the most popular knit fabrics used for lingerie. They drape nicely, and have a silk-like appearance. They are usually very easy to wash and care for as well, and available in a good range of solid colours and attractive prints. The sheer type of tricot is suitable for pants and bras, and as a decorative second layer on nightgowns and slips. Opaque tricots can be used for all types of lingerie including slips.

Some tricot type dress fabrics may be used successfully for lingerie, but often it is difficult to tell the right side of these fabrics. To be sure you have the right side, pull the fabric on the crosswise edge. The fabric will roll towards the right side.

Stretch lace fabrics combine the delicate sheerness of lace with a close-to-the-body fit. They are excellent for all types of lingerie.

Lightweight polyester lawns also make beautiful lingerie, so do lightweight rayon or rayon blend linings, and cotton batiste.

Hints to help

1. Scissors must be sharp to cut knits and slippery woven fabrics accurately without 'chewing' them.
2. Always use fine, good-quality dressmaker's pins.
3. For machine stitching use a size 9 or 11 needle. For knits, use a fine ball-point needle designed especially for sewing knits. Always use polyester threads for sewing synthetic wovens as these threads 'give' easily.
4. If you are using elastic, then use proper lingerie elastic which has a finished lacy edge on one side and is softer and more resilient than ordinary elastics.
5. Bra and slip straps can be purchased in most haberdashery departments, and so can special hook and eye attachments for bras.
6. When starting to machine-stitch knit fabrics, hold the ends of thread taut in the back of the machine needle. This keeps the fabric from being pulled down into the hole in the throat plate of the machine.
7. If you are using a sheer woven fabric, then stitch all seams with a French seam (see page 31), or a double-stitched seam (see page 31).
8. It is easier to attach elastic to a garment if you leave one side seam of the garment open so that you can work with it flat. Divide elastic and waistline edge into eight equal parts; mark with pins. Pin elastic to wrong side of garment, placing either the straight or the fancy edge along seamline, matching pin marks. Stitch close to this edge of elastic, stretching gently while stitching. Trim seam allowance under elastic close to stitching. Turn elastic to right side. Stitch close to other edge, matching pin marks. Stitch remaining seam of garment.

A gathered frill round the edge of the wrap-around skirt gives extra beach appeal to this holiday outfit of bathing suit, top and skirt.

Coping with difficult fabrics

SHEERS

Sheers generally fall into three categories: soft sheers such as chiffon; semi-soft sheers such as voile; crisp sheers such as organdie.

First make sure you choose the right pattern for your fabric, deciding the effect you want to achieve beforehand. As a general guide, it is a good idea to select designs cut on gently fitting lines with plenty of fullness and the minimum of seams and darts. Patterns designed especially for sheers are the best choice. Once you have chosen your fabric and pattern, then decide on your underlining and interfacing.

The underlining should be chosen with great care to give depth, interest and opaqueness without altering the lightness of your dress fabric. Suitable lining fabrics include soft Tricel and Dicel taffeta, polyester and cotton voile and lawn. For the best effect, the fibre content of the underlining should be the same as that of the dress. If a floating look is required, decide on a loose separate lining; if you want a light, fitted look, for instance, on the bodice if a dress, mount the fabric on to the lining, basting edges together and treating the two layers as one fabric. As a general rule, skirts are better loose lined, but the bodice and its lining should be handled as one.

Skirt hems on sheers may be either very wide or very narrow according to the lines and drape of the fabric. On a straight or full gathered skirt, a double fold hem is often effective. This type of finish adds weight to the hemline and improves the hang of the skirt, eliminating the turned raw edge that would normally show through. To make a hem this way, simply double the hem allowance: for instance, if you want a 4-in. hem, allow 8in. Turn up a 4-in. hem and press; then turn up 4in. again. Slip-stitch in place slipping the needle inside the fold between the stitches to conceal the stitching.

When the hemline is circular or flared, a narrow machine-stitched hem is usually preferable. Cut edge of fabric evenly, then to prevent the fabric fraying stitch $\frac{1}{8}$in. from raw edge. Turn under raw edge on line of stitching and turn under again, to the same width. Baste and then stitch in place. Hem the sheer fabric and the lining separately to avoid sagging and to prevent the sheer fabric from blousing over the underlining.

Because sheers tend to slip around avoid a smooth surface for cutting out. A cork or felt surface is best, or a cotton sheet placed under the fabric on your usual cutting table will make a good substitute. Sheers may also be kept smooth by pinning to tissue paper before cutting out. Use fine steel pins or, better still, long glass-headed pins, when pinning your pattern to the fabric. Always transfer pattern markings and construction symbols to sheers with tailor's tacks (see page 26).

Basic patterns, made up in sparkling and glitter fabrics, can be instantly transformed into glamour party outfits.

Warm for winter, chunky jacket is made up in a long-haired fur fabric, with toggle fastening.

Hints to help

1. Use a fine thread suitable for the fabric you are using.
2. Use a new, very fine sharp needle—a number 11 is ideal, with a 15 to 20 stitch length on your machine. The pressure exerted by the presser foot on the fabric should be light, no heavier than needed to carry the fabric gently and evenly under the foot.
3. Very sheer fabrics require gentle support when stitching—hold the seam at the back of the presser foot, gently guiding it through the machine.
4. Unstitched darts, gathers and shirring are generally more pleasing in a sheer fabric than the conventional stitched darts.
5. The ideal seam for use on sheer fabrics is the French seam see page 31).
6. If your garment requires a zipper, choose a lightweight nylon zipper. Often press studs and/or lightweight buttons with loop fastenings are more suitable for the fabric than a zipper.

FUR FABRICS

There are many types of fur fabrics available, ranging from the short-hair variety such as leopard, pony and zebra to the thick or long-hair type such as lamb, sheep, bear and mink. All fabrics that imitate fur should be treated as 'one-way' fabrics and the pattern pieces laid on with their tops all pointing in the same direction so the hairs of the fabric will run in the same direction.

If the fabric is very heavy it will usually be more satisfactory to cut it out with a razor blade instead of your usual cutting shears.

Choose a simple pattern when using fur fabric, with as few darts and seams as possible.

With thick or long-hair fabrics, it is best to trim hairs within the seam allowance before sewing, then baste seams firmly smoothing hair away from seams.

Use a medium size machine needle, a fairly long stitch, a loosened tension and mercerised thread. After stitching, pick hair out of seam with a pin. Slash all darts open.

To press, use a velvet board or several thicknesses of towels and press with a steam iron and press cloth.

On some of the thicker fur fabrics, you may not achieve a fine sharp line when pressing seams and edges. Therefore do not press, but instead place a cloth over seams and edges and pound them with a heavy object.

Worked or machine-made buttonholes may be made in short-hair fur fabrics. For longer furs, use button and chain closures or frogging fastenings (bought ready-made from haberdashery departments).

VELVET

Velvet is a wonderful luxury fabric. It can range in type from flock velvet and brocade velvet in which parts of the background are almost transparent and the pile is concentrated either in spot form or in a cluster of design, to chiffon and silk velvet which are expensive and gloriously soft and rich. Panne velvet has either a woven or knitted backing on it, and cotton, rayon and nylon velvets are usually combinations of various fibres. Most velvets should be dry-cleaned although washable velvets are available—usually mixtures of 80 per cent nylon with 20 per cent cotton.

Velvet for dressmaking should always be cut with the pile running upwards from hem to shoulder, and from wrist to armhole. If it is difficult to tell which way the pile is running, try placing the fabric over one shoulder round the neck and draping it on your left side, allowing it to fall to the ground. Look down upon it and the darker side is the right side up.

Place the velvet on the cutting table, and run the palm of your hand over its surface. The smooth way up is the run of the pile, and as the run should go upwards on the wrong side, arrow mark this with tailor's chalk to avoid any mistake when placing pattern pieces on the fabric.

Place the pattern pieces with the tops all running in the same direction. It is usually advisable to increase all seam allowances to 1in., instead of the usual $\frac{5}{8}$in. Take especial care when pinning velvet as pin marks will not disappear when the pins are removed: pin within the seam allowance, and within dart areas.

When you machine-stitch velvet, if you find that the layers of fabric tend to move and distort the seams, this can be overcome by placing tissue paper between the layers of velvet to keep the piles separate before you begin to stitch. The paper is simply torn away after stitching is complete. Always machine-stitch with the pile and not against it. Before pressing gently brush the piles out from the seam. If any unpicking should be necessary, unpick gently so as not to cut the ground fibres. Remove all the machine thread. Brush well. Steam the section and brush against the pile, then with the pile in a circular movement.

Before you press velvet, run your finger with a thimble on it along the seamline to open it up. To avoid the impression of the seamline showing through on to the right side of the garment, place a strip of brown paper (not newspaper) under each side of the seam as you press.

A finished garment will benefit from being hung up in a steamy bathroom for a few hours. Brush pile upwards.

LEATHER AND SUEDE
The selection and handling of skin requires special care and attention, but these 'fabrics' make fashions of classic and enduring beauty, so it is worth spending time getting to know and understand the sewing techniques involved.

Skin by its very nature is hard-wearing so it is therefore not too much to assume that it will wear for at least a few seasons. Consequently the seam construction should also stand up to the hard wear which is expected from a good-quality garment. Always use a heavy-duty, strong mercerised thread, a long stitch length (8–10 stitches per inch) and a new machine needle size 14–16 or a special leather needle. The tension of your machine should be slightly loose.

Choose a pattern which is simply styled with few seams and darts—avoid particularly short wide darts and curved seaming.

Leather and suede are sold as individual skins. Select skins which are uniform in weight and shade—your pattern will tell you how many skins you will need.

Hints to help

1. Never fold skins—lay the complete pattern on a single layer of skin to plan how and where to cut.

2. Pin marks will show, so pin well within the seam allowance, or attach pattern pieces to skin with self-adhesive transparent tape. Mark construction details with chalk on the wrong side.

3. With suede cut with tops of all pieces pointing to neck of the skin.

4. If skin is not wide enough to make a complete front or back, cut two separate pieces and seam in the centre. Remember to add on seam allowances when cutting.

5. With smooth leather, place pattern pieces all lengthwise or crosswise on right side of skins.

6. Stitching errors will show. Stitch with care to avoid ripping. Do not stretch as you stitch.

7. Do not pin seams—use paper clips, or tape to hold layers together. Do not back stitch. Tie thread ends to finish.

8. If the skin sticks or slips when you are stitching, place a piece of tissue paper under the work, or else rub talcum powder on top layer of the skin on the seam allowance.

9. Plain seams will 'roll' as they cannot be pressed flat with an iron. To keep seams flat after clipping, glue the seam allowance to the backing of the fabric with rubber adhesive.

10. Never steam-press. Press with a warm dry iron over a press cloth or sheet of strong brown paper.

VINYL

Vinyl is a useful and attractive novelty fashion fabric: its waterproof surface makes it a natural for rainwear, but it is also popular for bags, hats, scarves and aprons.

There are three principal types of vinyl:

1. Vinyl-coated fabrics. A clear film of vinyl coats a woven fabric, which is generally a plain-weave print or solid colour in cotton or nylon.

2. Transparent vinyl. A clear and colourless film without a backing.

3. Opaque vinyl. A thin film of printed or coloured vinyl is laminated to a backing of soft, flexible knit, usually cotton. The outer surface may be shiny, patent vinyl, or the surface may have a satin or matt finish. The dull finish is popular in fluorescent colours.

In general, follow instructions and hints for leather and suede, as given above, for all three types of vinyl.

KNIT FABRICS

These are among the newest additions to the fashion fabric story. They are wonderful for today's easy-care, freedom line clothes. Knits are available in a vast range of weights, types and colours: there's a knit to take you anywhere and everywhere!

To keep up with the knit revolution there are now available: special stretch threads that 'give' with the fabric, made of polyester; the ball-point needle with a slightly rounded point that will not damage knits; the new invisible zipper with the nylon teeth which is lightweight and flexible; featherweight polyester non-woven interfacing that also 'gives' like the knit fabric. Many sewing machines are equipped with a number of

Classic princess-style dress to suit all occasions has top-stitching detail and mock pockets.

special stretch stitches to simplify sewing these stretchy fabrics.

Knit fabrics are made of interlocking loops, a construction that gives them greater flexibility than that found in woven fabrics. There are two types of knit fabrics: single and double. Single knits are made with only one yarn and may be circular or flat. Double knits consist of two layers of fabric knitted together with two sets of needles and two or more layers of yarns. Wool, cotton, synthetics or blends of two or more kinds of yarn are used in both single and double knits.

Before laying out your fabric press a section of the lengthwise fold, if there is one, to see if it can be removed. If not, avoid placing pattern pieces on the fold. Knits do not have a grainline like woven fabrics, but many have noticeable lengthwise ribs. To lay out, follow ribs as you would a lengthwise grain, placing the grainline of the pattern straight in this direction. The lengthwise of a knit is usually the most stable direction.

Use sharp pins and shears. Do not let fabric hang over the edge of the cutting surface.

Seams must have some 'give' especially in armholes and crosswise seams. Stitch a test seam to determine the best one for your fabric. If you are using a machine with stretch stitch, use a multiple stitch zigzag for seams and finishing edges, and an elastic straight stitch for seams.

To get stretch into seams of very lightweight knits, try a stitched and pulled seam: loosen tension on machine; stitch seam leaving 4in. of thread at one end. After the seam is stitched ease with fingers the excess thread into the seam, stretching a small distance each time.

To stretch as you stitch the seam, hold fabric with left hand in back of presser foot and right hand in front, stretching gently while stitching. Avoid over-stretching. Top-stitching may be necessary to keep seam allowances flat on the crosswise seams of tricots. If seam allowances tend to fray or curl, zigzag with regular or multiple-stitch zigzag. To stabilise shoulder and waistline seams, stitch straight seam tape into them.

Let garments hang for twenty-four hours before hemming. The catch-stitched hem is the best hemming method to use for knits (see page 33).

If possible always choose patterns that are specially recommended for knit fabrics. Although fashion allows less ease for knit garments, to be attractive they should not look tight or over-fitted. Because the fabric gives, the garment may feel comfortable, but still be too tight. You should fit a double knit closer to the body than the soft, drapable knits which look better in a looser fit. You may find that a pattern made in a knit fits differently than when made in a woven fabric.

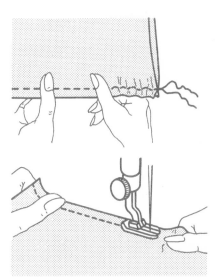

CHECKS AND PLAIDS

Plaids, checks and even stripes present certain problems when it comes to making them up but if you spend a little time beforehand on planning out the placing of your pattern pieces, you should have no trouble.

As there is inevitably more wastage with one of these fabrics than with a plain one, extra yardage will be necessary. Most commercial paper patterns will quote how much extra fabric you should buy to allow for matching checks and stripes. If this

Wardrobe of mix-and-match separates, suitable for knit fabrics.

is not given, then add $\frac{1}{8}$ yard for a small plaid or check, $\frac{1}{4}$ to $\frac{1}{2}$ yard for a medium-sized check, and up to 1 yard for a large check. Choose a pattern with a minimum number of pattern pieces and seams, and with simple unbroken lines.

Avoid circular yokes, gored skirts and styles with wide or draped sleeves. It is best to cut all the pattern pieces from single thickness fabric so you can see exactly how the check pattern will fall. But do not forget to reverse a pattern piece for the second cutting.

To match one side of the garment to the other, first establish a suitable area of the check design for the first side, then pin the pattern piece in position to the fabric, and using a soft lead pencil trace the check design of the fabric on to the tissue pattern. When this piece is cut out the pattern is simply placed on a second area of fabric to correspond with the lines marked from the first piece.

Try to match checks and stripes at the following points: on a bodice, blouse or one-piece dress match crosswise bars at side seam notches, along centre front and centre back seams. If there is an underarm dart, side seams will only match from the dart down. Match collars at centre back seam to the centre back of garment.

Striped fabrics are as a rule easier to handle than plaid and check fabrics because the design runs in only one direction— lengthwise or crosswise—and therefore need be matched or arranged in only one direction.

There are two types of stripes: even and uneven. No problem exists in cutting even stripes. You need only observe the ordinary precautions of laying matching parts on the same stripes. Uneven stripes must be cut as you would cut a 'one-way' fabric with the tops of the pieces pointing in the same direction. When working with uneven lengthwise stripes you may plan to arrange the stripes to move in opposite directions from the centre (a balanced effect) or to follow right around the figure.

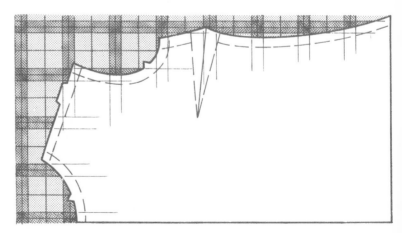

The patterns

A wardrobe of classic clothes to make for you and your family, based on the sewing techniques described in the preceding chapters.

MAKING YOUR PAPER PATTERN

Each outfit to make in this chapter is presented here in the form of a diagram pattern: a miniature pattern worked out to scale on a squared background or grid. It is a simple matter to convert these miniature patterns to give you a full-size pattern.

You will need several large sheets of strong brown or white paper. Using your yardstick and a sharp, fairly hard pencil mark out the total area of the paper into 1-in. squares. Most diagram patterns are presented on a 1-in. grid—i.e. each square on the miniature pattern represents one square inch in actual size.

Sometimes however a pattern will be on a 2-in. grid, or even a $\frac{1}{2}$-in. grid. Check to see what scale the pattern you are following uses, and then mark out your paper accordingly—if the grid is 2 in., then mark out your paper into 2-in. squares; alternatively, if the grid is only $\frac{1}{2}$in., then mark your paper into $\frac{1}{2}$-in. squares.

Now check the size of the pattern as given on the miniature grid. If you are a size bigger than the size quoted—e.g. if the pattern is for bust size 34in., hip size 36in., and you are bust size 36in., hip size 38in.—then the pattern will have to be adjusted accordingly. Add $\frac{1}{2}$in. to all side seams (giving a total of 2in. altogether), and draw in these new side edges on the miniature pattern (remember that if the pattern is on a 1-in. grid, then half a square will equal $\frac{1}{2}$in.).

If there are other pattern pieces which relate to the side edges of the garment these will have to be adjusted as well. For instance a belt pattern piece will have to have 2in. added to its length. A sleeve facing, or head of a sleeve which sets into the armhole will have to have 1in. added to its length (add the extra measurement at underarm seam—in the case of a sleeve add the extra measurement at underarm seam where sleeve sets into armhole, then gradually taper new cutting line from this point to meet original cutting line of sleeve).

If the pattern is a size too big for you, of course, you will have to deduct the appropriate amount from side edges, and other edges related to the side edges.

When you are satisfied the miniature pattern is basically correct for your size—further minor adjustments can be made once you have a full-size pattern prepared just as you would with a bought paper pattern (see chapter beginning on page 45)—then copy the pattern from the miniature grid on to your squared paper. Each of the squares on the small grid represents one full-size square on your prepared grid. Follow the outlines and positions of all curves and lines in relation to the squares as accurately as possible.

Facing sections and often pockets are usually shown on the miniature diagram as shaded areas. Prepare separate pattern pieces on your grid for all these pieces.

Now transfer the marks, notches, arrows and instructions from the miniature diagram on to your full-size pattern pieces.

Write on the name of each pattern piece—e.g. Bodice Front, Skirt Back, Sleeve, and so on—as well as a general name for the particular outfit so you will know afterwards what the pattern is for. For instance, 'Long-sleeved Winter Dress', or 'Three-piece Classic Suit'. Cut out all pattern pieces, and you are ready to cut out your fabric, and proceed with the making of your outfit just as you would using a bought paper pattern.

*Top-fashion cape in checked wool tweed—
making instructions on page 167.*

Baby's angel top

MATERIALS
$\frac{3}{4}$yd. of fabric, 36in. wide, or $\frac{5}{8}$yd. fabric, 45in. wide; 12in. of narrow elastic; 5ft. lace edging, $\frac{3}{4}$in. wide; 2 small buttons.

FABRIC SUGGESTION
Our angel top was made up in a self-striped cotton lawn in pink, and trimmed with white ready-gathered lace edging.

SIZE NOTE
The pattern as given will comfortably fit a baby of about 6 months; centre back length is 10$\frac{1}{2}$in.; neck measurement is 10$\frac{1}{2}$in. To adapt the pattern to fit a bigger or smaller size, see page 106.

TO MAKE YOUR PATTERN
The diagram on page 111 gives the pattern pieces you need. One square on the diagram equals 1in. Prepare your full-size pattern on squared paper, following instructions on page 106. Cut out fabric, following cutting-out layouts on page 110. Place dress front on fold of fabric, as indicated, to avoid a seam at this point in the garment. Cut a rouleau strip 1$\frac{1}{8}$in. by 12in. for neck edging.
Unless otherwise stated, all seams should be stitched $\frac{5}{8}$in. from the edge of fabric; press all seams open after stitching.

TO MAKE
On each back section, fold back fabric to wrong side along fold line as marked on pattern. Press.
Make two worked buttonholes on left back in positions indicated. Right sides together, stitch front to backs at side edges. Right sides together, stitch underarm seam in each sleeve. Fold lower edge of each sleeve to wrong side along fold line as marked on pattern. Turn in raw edge and make two rows of stitching as marked on pattern, leaving seam open. Cut elastic in half and insert one length into each cuff, through channel just stitched. Stitch ends of elastic together, and stitch seam closed. Stitch sleeves to dress, right sides together, along raglan edges, matching notches.
Work two rows of gathering stitches right round neck edge, and draw gathers up evenly until neck edge is 11$\frac{1}{2}$in.
Fold rouleau strip in half lengthwise, right sides together, and stitch across each short end. Trim seam. Turn right side out, and right sides together pin round neck edge of dress. Stitch, adjusting gathers evenly, and only stitching through dress fabric and one layer of the rouleau. Trim and clip seam. Turn in seam allowance on other edge of rouleau and slip-stitch neatly by hand to inside of neck edge seam just stitched.

Top: baby's angel top. Below: child's cotton dress (see page 112).

Turn up and stitch a narrow hem round lower edge. Stitch lace trimming right round this edge, and also round lower edge of each sleeve. Overlap left back over right back so centre back points line up (see marking on pattern piece). Mark positions of buttonholes on right back and sew a button at each of these points.

(**Note.** If the fabric is fine, it would be advisable to use French seams.)

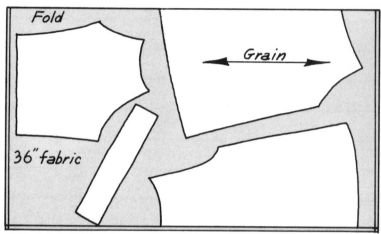

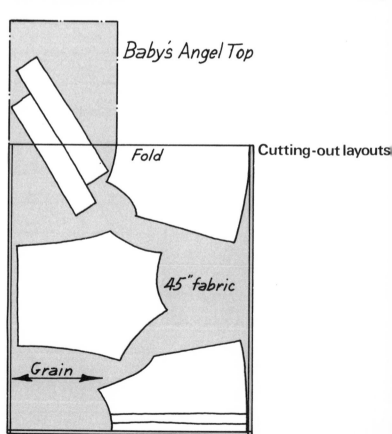

Baby's Angel Top

Cutting-out layouts

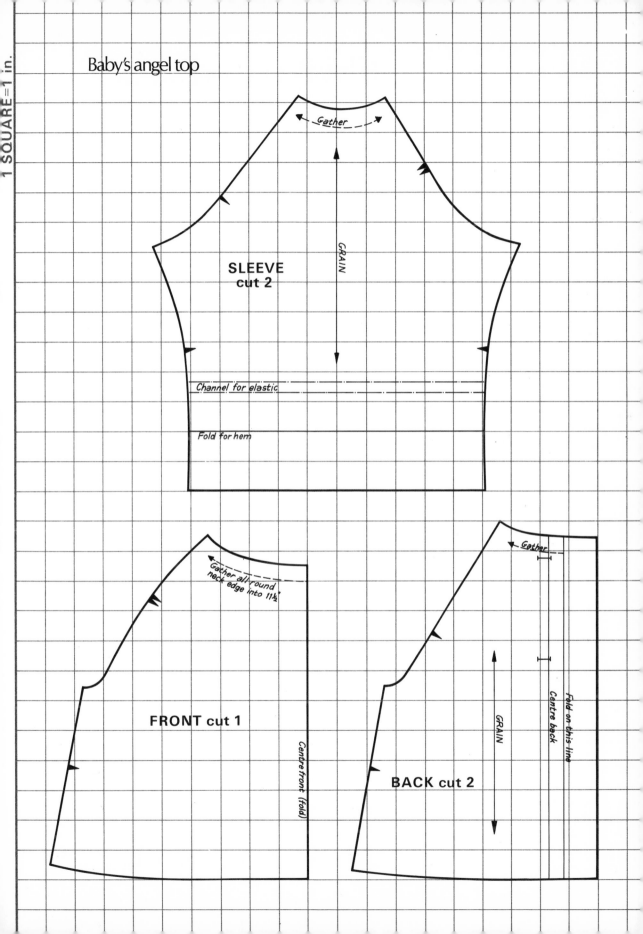

1 SQUARE=1 in.

Baby's angel top

SLEEVE
cut 2

GRAIN

Gather

Channel for elastic

Fold for hem

FRONT cut 1

Gather all round
neck edge into 11½"

Centre front (fold)

BACK cut 2

Gather

GRAIN

Fold on this line

Centre back

Child's cotton dress

illustrated in colour on page 108

MATERIALS

$1\frac{7}{8}$yd. of fabric, 36in. wide, or $1\frac{1}{2}$yd. of fabric, 54 in. wide; a 12-in. zipper; 1 hook and eye; $\frac{1}{2}$yd. narrow elastic.

FABRIC SUGGESTION

Our dress is made up in a printed cotton pique.

SIZE NOTE

The pattern as given will comfortably fit a girl of about six years old, with a chest measurement of 24/26in.; centre back length is 22in.; sleeve seam 12in. To adapt the pattern to fit a bigger or smaller size, see page 106.

TO MAKE YOUR PATTERN

The diagram on pages 114–5 gives the pieces you need. One square on the diagram equals 1in. Prepare your full-size pattern on squared paper, following instructions on page 106. Cut out fabric, following cutting-out layouts opposite. Place dress front on fold of fabric, as indicated, to avoid a seam at this point in the garment. Cut collar on the cross of the fabric, as indicated. Unless otherwise stated, all seams should be stitched $\frac{5}{8}$in. from the edge of fabric; press all seams open after stitching.

TO MAKE

Make tucks on dress front as indicated on pattern piece, by taking solid lines to dotted lines (see page 66). Bring folds at either side of centre front together at centre front and stitch. Press tuck folds flat on the wrong side of fabric. Right sides together, stitch dress back sections together at centre back, leaving seam open from neck edge down as indicated on pattern, for the zipper. Insert zipper to this seam. Right sides together, stitch dress back to dress front as shoulders and side edges.

Fold collar in half lengthwise. Stitch across each short end. Trim and clip seam, turn collar right side out.

Right sides together, pin collar in position to neck edge of dress. stitching through dress fabric and one layer of the collar only. Layer and clip seam. Turn in seam allowance along remaining open edge of collar, and slip-stitch over seam just stitched on wrong side of dress. If wished, a row of top-stitching can be worked right along neck edge seam, through all layers of fabric. Let collar double over to form a roll collar.

Right sides together, stitch underarm seam in each sleeve. Gather round head of sleeve as marked on pattern piece. Fold lower edge of sleeve to wrong side at fold line marked on pattern. Turn in seam allowance and make two rows of stitching, as marked on pattern, leaving a gap in the seam. Cut elastic into two equal lengths and thread one length through each cuff, through channel just stitched. Stitch ends of elastic together, and stitch seam closed. Set sleeves into armholes of dress, matching notches. Turn up lower hem to length required, and stitch neatly. Sew hook and eye to fasten centre back at neck edge above zipper.

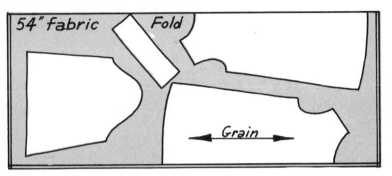

Child's Cotton Dress

Cutting-out layouts

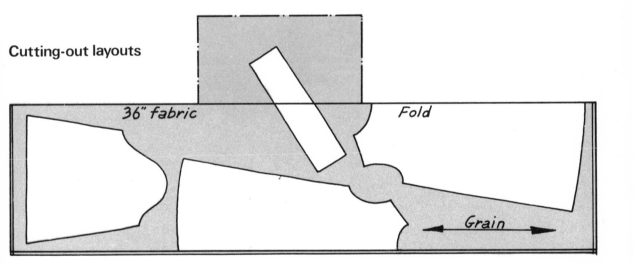

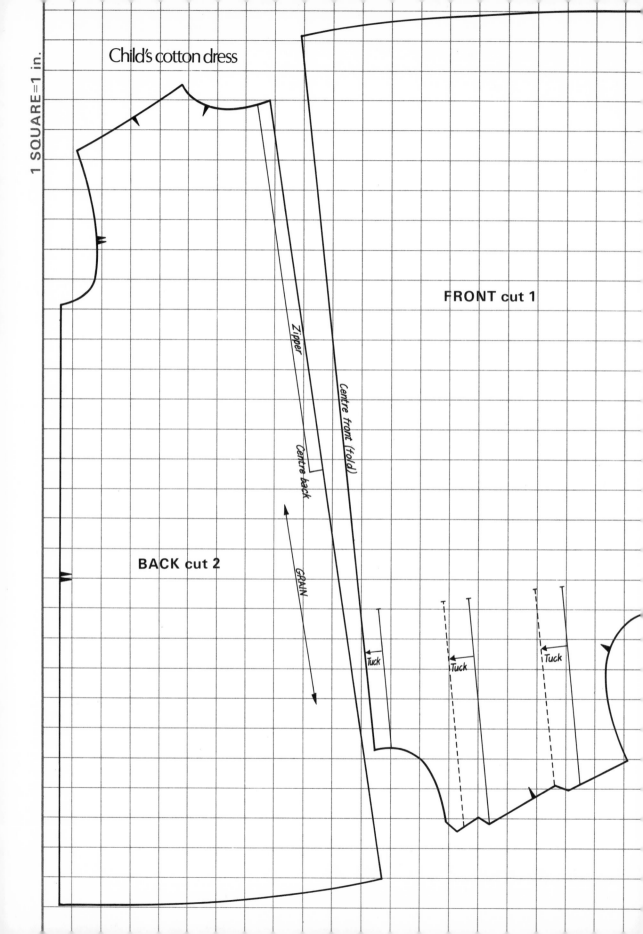

1 SQUARE=1 in.

Child's cotton dress

FRONT cut 1

Zipper

Centre front (fold)

Centre back

GRAIN

BACK cut 2

Tuck

Tuck

Tuck

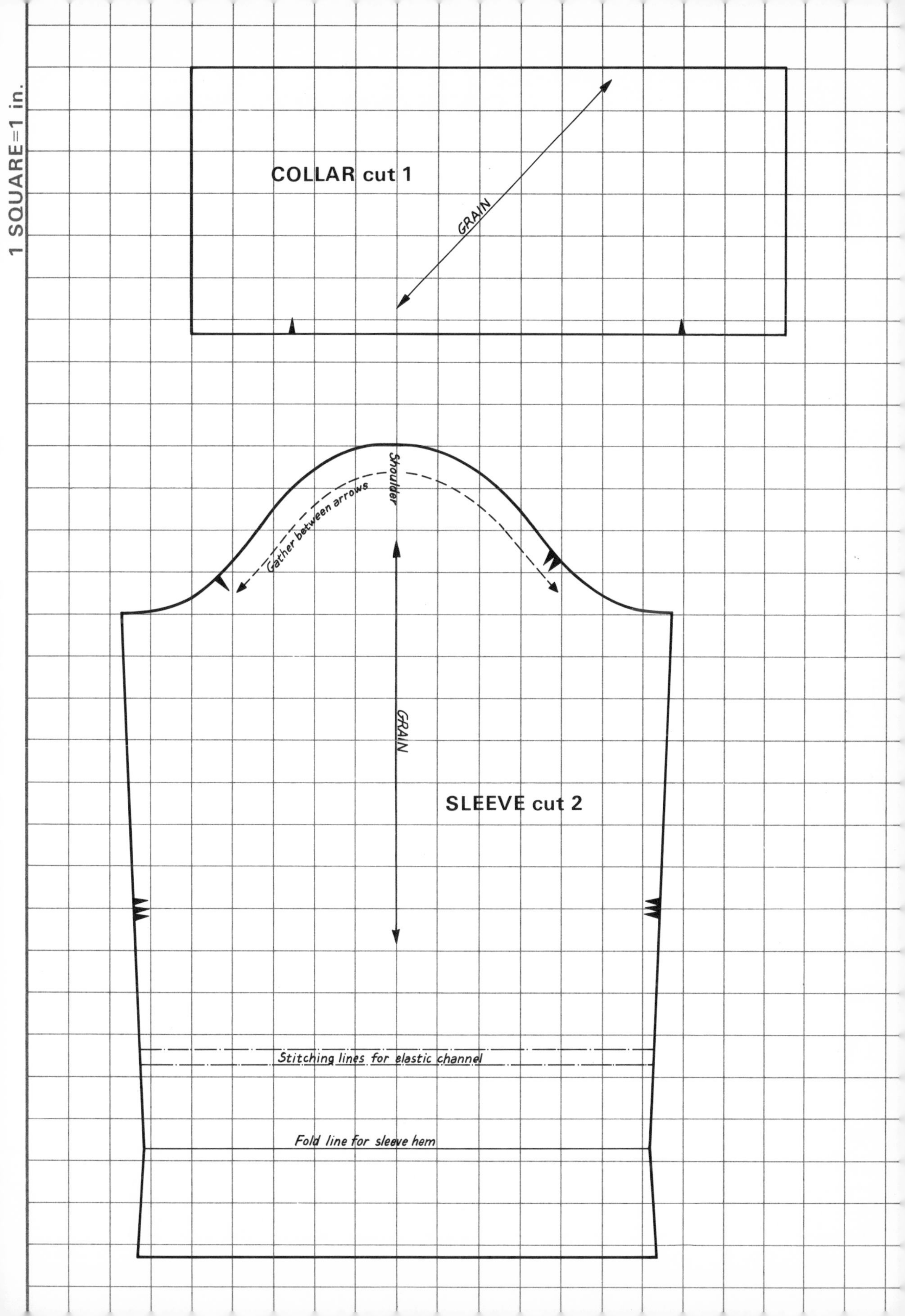

1 SQUARE=1 in.

COLLAR cut 1

GRAIN

Shoulder

Gather between arrows

GRAIN

SLEEVE cut 2

Stitching lines for elastic channel

Fold line for sleeve hem

Child's dressing-gown

illustrated on page 125

MATERIALS

$2\frac{1}{2}$yd. of fabric, 36in. wide, or 2yd. of fabric, 54in. wide.

FABRIC SUGGESTION

Our dressing-gown is made up in a soft cotton molleton (a mediumweight fabric with a warm brushed finish).

SIZE NOTE

The pattern as given will comfortably fit a child of about six years old, with a chest measurement of about 26in.; centre back length is 26in.; sleeve seam 10in. To adapt the pattern to fit a bigger or smaller size, see page 106.

TO MAKE YOUR PATTERN

The diagram on pages 118–9 gives the pieces you need. One square on the diagram equals 1in. Prepare your full-size pattern on squared paper, following instructions on page 106. Cut out fabric, following cutting-out layouts opposite. Place back and belt on fold of fabric, as indicated, to avoid a seam at these points in the garment.

Cut 2 strips of fabric, each $3\frac{1}{2}$ by 1in., for belt carriers. Unless otherwise stated, all seams should be stitched $\frac{5}{8}$in. from the edge of fabric; press all seams open after stitching.

TO MAKE

Right sides together, stitch front sections together at short seam at very top of pattern piece (this section, above shoulder seams, forms the back collar of dressing-gown).

Right sides together stitch front to back at side seams and shoulder edges. Clip into inner corner of each shoulder seam on dressing-gown fronts as marked on pattern piece. clipping almost as far as the stitching.

Right sides together, stitch neck edges of collar section and back together.

Right sides together stitch facings together at short seam (centre back neck) at top of pattern piece.

Right sides together pin facings in place to dressing-gown centre front edges and round back neck. Stitch. Layer and clip seam and turn facings to inside of gown. Turn in seam allowance at shoulder and back neck edges and slip-stitch neatly by hand over seams already stitched. Neaten remaining raw edges of facing down each side of front opening.

Right sides together, stitch underarm seam of each sleeve, then stitch sleeves into armholes of gown, matching notches. Fold lower edge of each sleeve to wrong side along fold line marked on pattern. Hem-stitch neatly in place.

Turn up lower hem to length required. Open out facings, and

stitch hem in place. Fold facings back and slip-stitch to hem along lower edge.

Make up two patch pockets, following instructions on page 42, and stitch to front of gown in positions indicated on pattern diagram.

To make belt, fold belt strip in half lengthwise, right sides together, and stitch right round open edges, leaving a gap in the seam to turn belt right side out. Turn right side out, turn in seam allowance on gap and slip-stitch opening closed. Press well.

To make belt carriers, fold each strip in half lengthwise, wrong sides together, turn in seam allowance on raw edges down long seam, and slip-stitch together. Press so seam runs down centre of strip. Fold back each short end for about $\frac{1}{2}$in. and stitch in place to right side of seams of gown at waist level.

If wished top-stitching may be worked round cuff edges (on hemline), round lower edge (on hemline), and round armhole seam, side seams and shoulder seams (all double rows of top-stitching).

Alternatively stitch all seams with a flat-felled seam for extra strength and a neat finished appearance.

Note. As this dressing-gown has no button fastenings on it, it may be made for either a boy or a girl. If made for a girl, then lap right front over left; if made for a boy then lap left front over right.

Cutting-out layouts

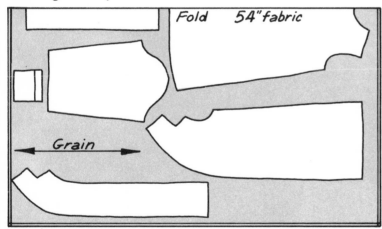

Child's Dressing-gown

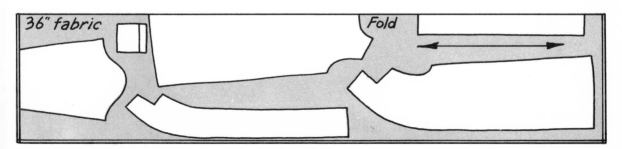

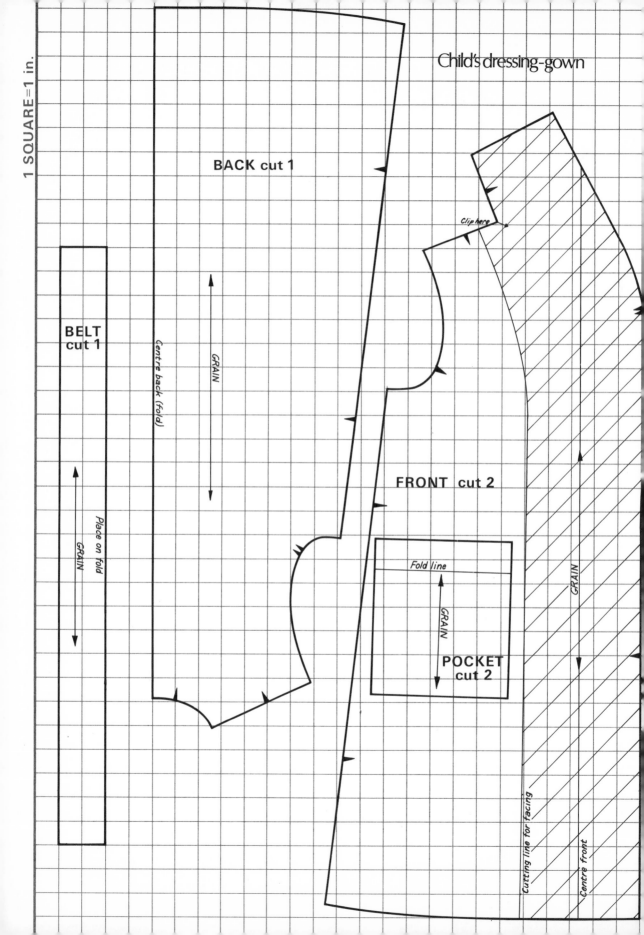

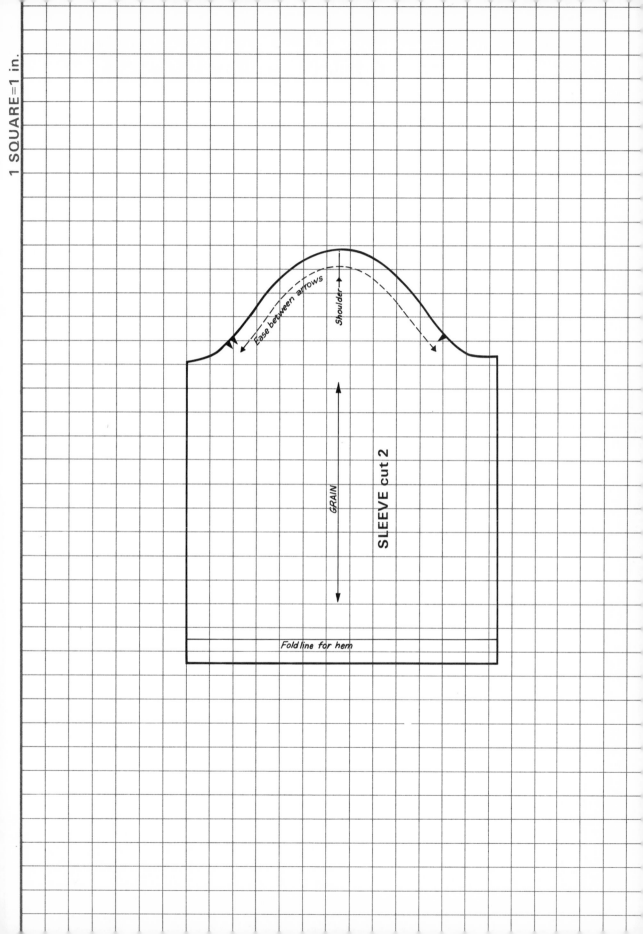

1 SQUARE=1 in.

Ease between arrows

Shoulder

GRAIN

SLEEVE cut 2

Fold line for hem

Child's quilted anorak

illustrated in colour on page 72

MATERIALS

1yd. of quilted, waterproof nylon, 54 or 58in. wide; 1⅝yd. of Tricel lining fabric; a 16-in. open-ended zipper; two ¾-in. silver buckles; 1yd. of mediumweight silk cord to match quilted fabric.

SIZE NOTE

The pattern as given will comfortably fit a child of about five/six years old, with a chest measurement of 26/28in.; centre back length (excluding hood) is 18in.; sleeve seam 11in. To adapt the pattern to fit a bigger or smaller size, see page 106.

TO MAKE YOUR PATTERN

The diagram on pages 122–3 gives the pieces you need. One square on the diagram equals 1in. Prepare your full-size pattern on squared paper, following instructions on page 106. Cut out fabric pieces, following cutting-out layouts opposite.

Place jacket back on fold of fabric as indicated to avoid a seam at this point in the garment.

Cut out lining pieces for front, back, sleeve, hood and pocket, following cutting lines indicated on main pattern pieces. Unless otherwise stated, all seams should be stitched ⅝in. from the edge of fabric; press all seams open after stitching.

TO MAKE

Right sides together, stitch jacket fronts to back at side seams. Stitch zip into centre front edges, having top of zip level with neck edge. Right sides together, stitch underarm seam of each sleeve. Right sides together, stitch each sleeve to jacket at raglan seams, matching notches. Turn up lower edge of each sleeve to length required and baste.

Right sides together, stitch hood sections together round curved edges (back of head). On right side of hood make two worked buttonholes as marked on pattern. Fold front (face) edge of hood to wrong side along fold line marked on pattern. Run a line of stitching right round this edge starting and finishing at neck edge, as marked on pattern.

Right sides together, stitch hood to neck edge of jacket, easing hood to fit. Stitch. Layer and clip seam. Press seam up. Turn up lower hem of jacket to length required and baste. In a similar way make up lining for jacket, stitching side seams first, then underarm seams of sleeves, then raglan seams, then curved seams in hood, then finally stitch hood to main section. Turn up hems at lower edges of sleeves, and round lower edges of front and back, and baste.

Wrong sides together, fit lining into jacket, placing lining into sleeves, and matching raglan seams. Before fitting lining into hood, catch-stitch lining to jacket right round neck edge.

Place hood lining in place, and slip-stitch lining to jacket round face edges of hood, down centre front edges, and right along lower hem edges. Slip-stitch lower edge of lining sleeves to hem of jacket sleeves.

Place one pocket lining section to one pocket fabric section, right sides together. Stitch round sides and lower edge. Trim and clip seam, and turn to right side, turn in seam allowance along top edge on lining and fabric and machine-stitch close to edge. Repeat with other pocket fabric and lining sections. Stitch each patch pocket in position to jacket front, as marked on pattern diagram.

To make each sleeve band, fold each strip of fabric in half lengthwise, letting one long edge overlap the other. Turn in raw edge down the uppermost long edge, and position so this fold runs down the centre of the strip. Machine-stitch down strip through all thicknesses, and keeping stitching close to edge of turned-in fold. Stitch one short end over the bar of one buckle. Turn in the other short end to about $\frac{1}{2}$in. and stitch across end to hold in place. Place band round sleeve about $1\frac{1}{2}$in. up from lower edge. Catch-stitch neatly to sleeve seam to hold in place.

Thread cord through casing round front edge of hood.

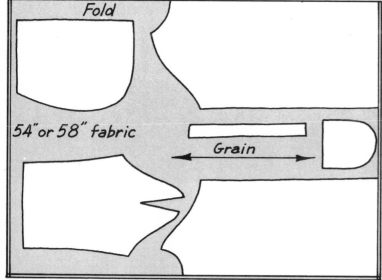

Cutting-out layouts

Child's Quilted Anorak

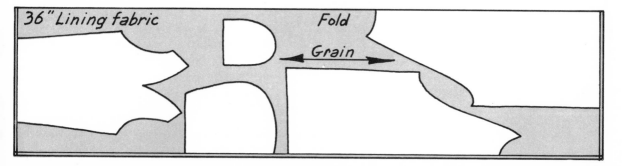

1 SQUARE=1 in.

Child's quilted anorak

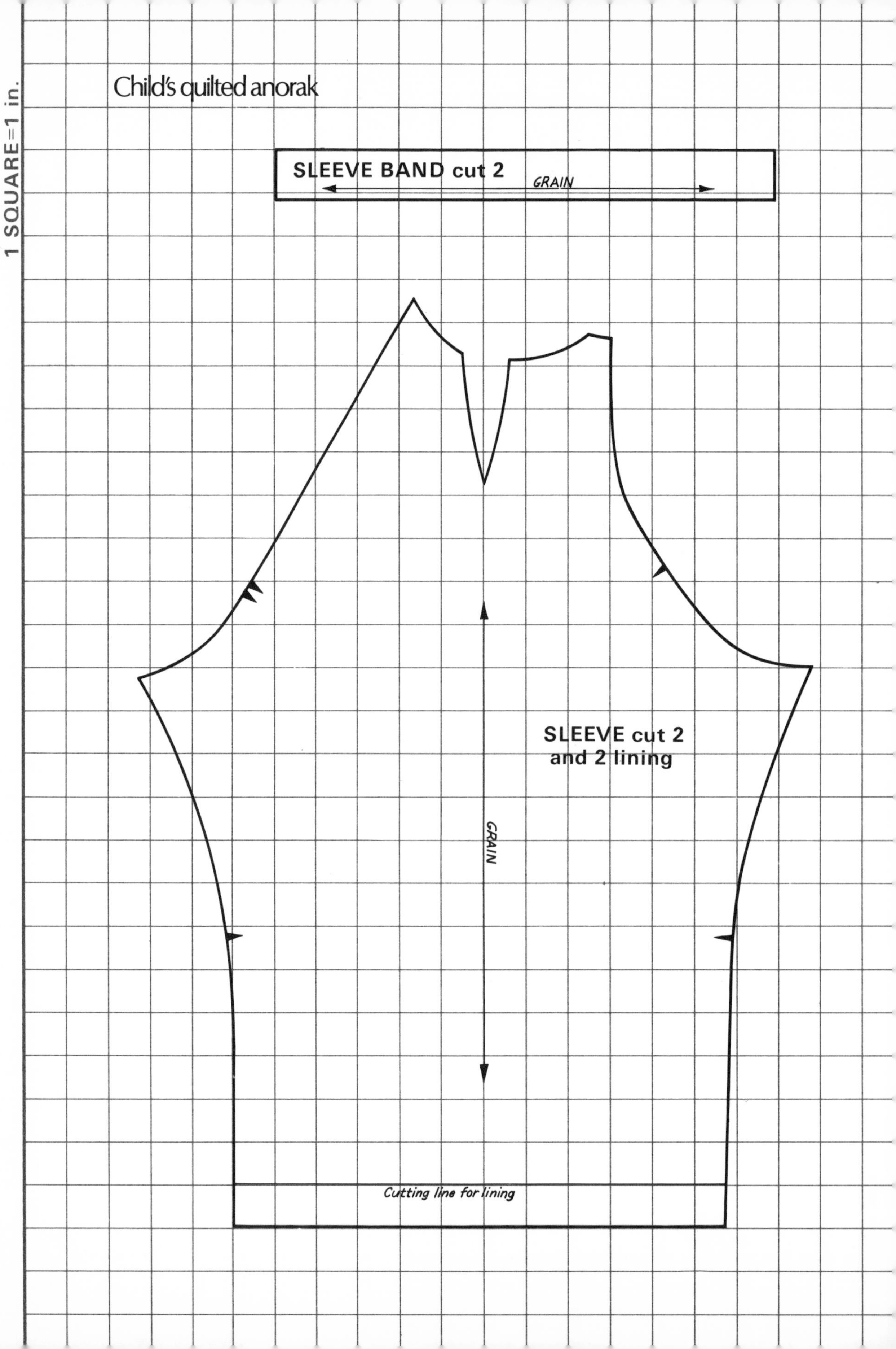

SLEEVE BAND cut 2   GRAIN

SLEEVE cut 2
and 2 lining

GRAIN

Cutting line for lining

1 SQUARE=1 in.

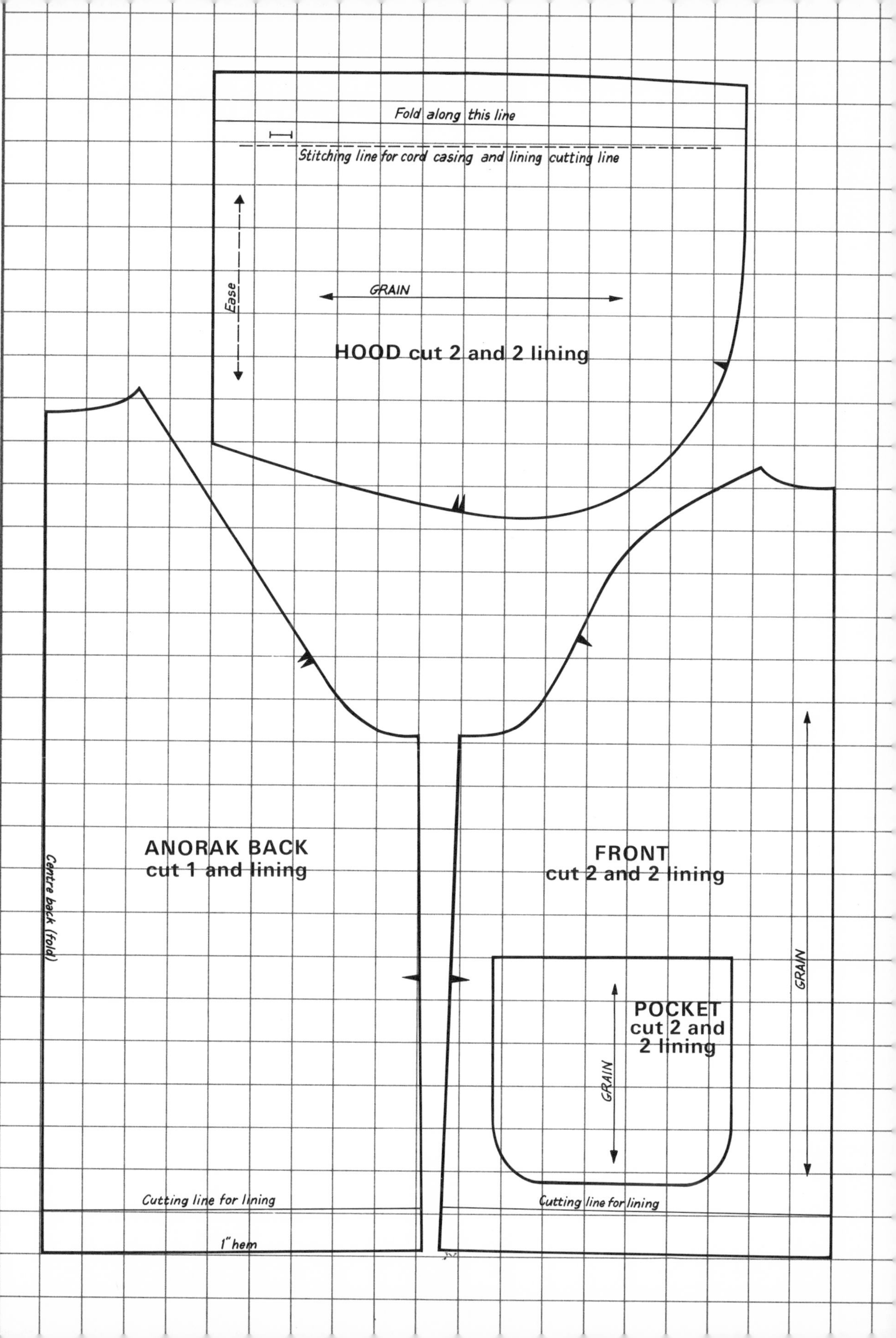

Fold along this line

Stitching line for cord casing and lining cutting line

Ease

GRAIN

HOOD cut 2 and 2 lining

**ANORAK BACK
cut 1 and lining**

Centre back (fold)

**FRONT
cut 2 and 2 lining**

GRAIN

**POCKET
cut 2 and
2 lining**

GRAIN

Cutting line for lining

Cutting line for lining

1" hem

Boy's shirt and trousers

MATERIALS
For shirt: $1\frac{3}{4}$yd. of fabric, 36in. wide; $\frac{1}{2}$yd. mediumweight interfacing, 32 or 36in. wide; eight $\frac{1}{2}$-in. buttons. **For trousers:** $1\frac{3}{4}$yd. of fabric, 36in. wide, or 1 yd. of fabric, 54in. wide; a waist length of elastic, $\frac{1}{2}$in. wide; a bought elastic, clasp-fastening belt.

FABRIC SUGGESTIONS
Our shirt was made in a plaid-patterned Viyella; the trousers in a mediumweight corduroy.

SIZE NOTE
The pattern as given will comfortably fit a boy of about six years old, with a chest measurement of about 26in.; centre back length of shirt is 21in.; sleeve seam (including cuff) 13in. Inside leg seam of trousers 17in.
To adapt the pattern to fit a bigger or smaller size, see page 106.

TO MAKE YOUR PATTERN
The diagram on pages 129–30 gives the pieces you need. One square on the diagram equals 1in. Prepare your full-size pattern on squared paper, following instructions on page 106. Cut out fabric, following cutting-out layouts on page 128. Place shirt back, collar and cuff pieces on fold as indicated, to avoid a seam at these points in the garment. Cut shirt pocket on the cross of the fabric as indicated.
From single thickness interfacing, cut out front facing twice, collar once and cuff twice. Cut out 4 strips of fabric, each $3\frac{1}{2}$ by $1\frac{1}{4}$in. for belt carriers on trousers.
Unless otherwise stated, all seams should be stitched $\frac{5}{8}$in. from the edge of the fabric; press all seams open after stitching.

TO MAKE
Shirt
Pin interfacing to wrong side of jacket shirt front facing sections. If using iron-on interfacing, then iron it on; if using sew-in interfacing then baste interfacing in place.
On each front section fold facing on to right side along fold line marked on the pattern. At neck edge, stitch from fold as far as centre front (this is only about $\frac{5}{8}$in.—see marking on pattern piece). Trim and clip seam. Turn in seam allowance on shoulder edge of facing, and baste. Press seam allowance of long raw edge of facing on to wrong side over interfacing. Machine-stitch close to folded edge.
Right sides together, join shirt fronts to back at shoulder and side edges: use a French seam for side seams; flat-felled seam for shoulder edges.

Above: child's dressing-gown (see page 116).
Left: boy's shirt and trousers.

On wrong side of collar iron on or baste on interfacing to one half of the section. Fold collar in half lengthwise, right sides together, and stitch down each short end. Trim and clip seam and turn collar right side out.

Having interfaced collar section as top collar, pin collar to right side of neck edge of shirt, matching notches. Overlap right side of front facings on to collar at each side, lining up neck edges evenly. Stitch, stitching through all fabric thicknesses at front of shirt as far as shoulder seams, then through undercollar and shirt only round back neck edge. Layer and clip seam, clipping almost to the stitching on collar seam allowance at shoulders.

Turn front facings to wrong side of shirt, carefully pushing neck edges into good sharp corners. Turn in seam allowance on remaining edge of collar round back neck, and slip-stitch neatly by hand to inside of seam just stitched.

Slip-stitch shoulder edge of front facings to inside of shirt shoulder seams. Make six worked buttonholes on left front, in positions marked on pattern piece.

Right sides together, and using a French seam, stitch each underarm seam in each sleeve. Cut slit in lower edge of each sleeve, as indicated on pattern piece.

Fold each sleeve placket strip in half lengthwise. Right sides together, pin to sleeve slit lining up raw edges. Stitch, stitching through sleeve fabric and a single layer of the placket strip only. Turn in seam allowance on remaining edge, and slip-stitch neatly by hand to the wrong side of seam just stitched. Press placket to wrong side along seam line. Baste short ends in position to cuff edges. Make two small pleats at lower edges of cuff as indicated on pattern, by folding on solid line and taking to broken line. Baste to hold in place. Iron on or baste on inter-facing to wrong side of each cuff, positioning interfacing on one half of cuff section only. Fold cuff in half lengthwise, right sides together, and stitch each short end. Trim and clip seams and turn right side out. Pin to lower edge of sleeve, having cuff edges at placket opening. Stitch, stitching through sleeve fabric and one layer of cuff only. Turn in seam allowance on remaining edge of cuff and slip-stitch neatly by hand to inside of seam just stitched. Make worked buttonhole in cuff as indicated on pattern piece.

Using a flat-felled seam, and matching notches, set sleeves into shirt armholes.

Make patch pockets, following instructions on page 42, and stitch to shirt front, in positions indicated on pattern diagram. Open out front facings, and turn up and stitch a narrow hem round lower edge. Fold facings back and slip-stitch neatly to hem along lower edge.

Lap left front over right front, lining up centre fronts. Mark buttonhole positions on right front, and sew a button at each of these markings. Sew a button to each cuff opposite button-hole worked.

Trousers

Using flat-felled seams, first join front sections together at centre front, then join back sections together at centre back. Join trousers front to trousers back at side seams, leaving right

Separates for day and evening—making instructions on page 158.

side seam open for pocket, as marked on pattern piece. Right sides together, stitch one pocket piece to each seam allowance. Turn pocket pieces to inside, press seam towards garment. Sew curved edges of pocket pieces together. Press pocket towards garment, clipping seam above and below pocket so it will lie flat. Fold waist edge to inside, along fold line marked. Turn in seam allowance on raw edge, then machine-stitch close to this folded edge, leaving a gap in the seam. Insert elastic into this casing, stitch ends of elastic together, and slip-stitch seam closed. Using a flat-felled seam, join inner leg seams.

Turn up lower hem at each leg to length required, and stitch neatly.

To make belt carriers, fold each strip in half lengthwise, wrong sides together. Turn in raw edges and work a row of machine stitching through all thicknesses of fabric down length of strip. Fold in short edges at each end for about $\frac{1}{2}$in. Stitch to right side of trousers at positions marked on pattern diagram.

Cutting-out layouts

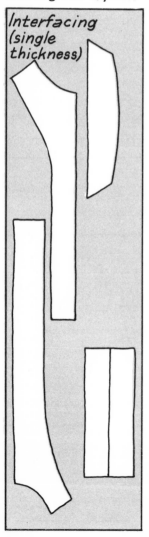

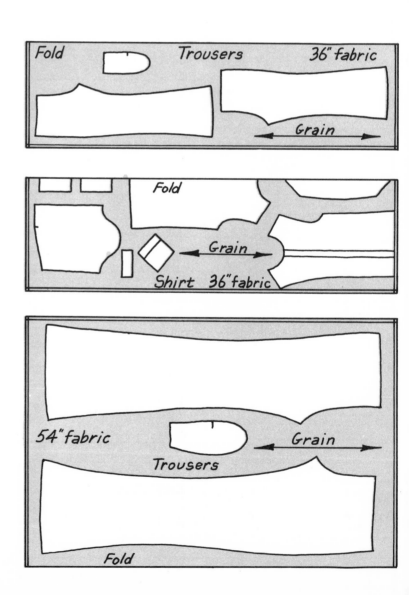

1 SQUARE=1 in.

Boy's shirt and trousers

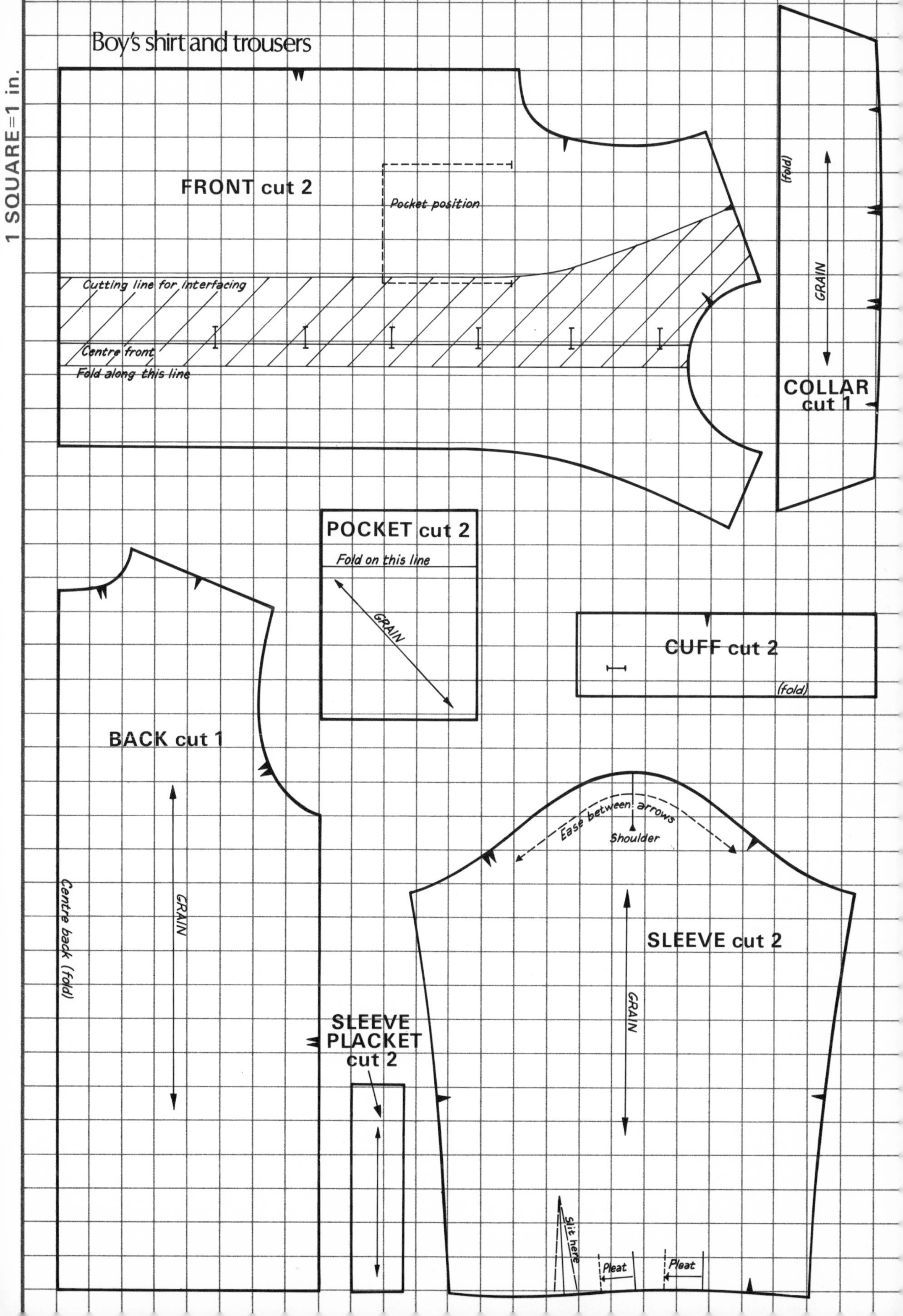

FRONT cut 2

Pocket position

Cutting line for interfacing

Centre front
Fold along this line

(fold)

GRAIN

COLLAR
cut 1

POCKET cut 2

Fold on this line

GRAIN

CUFF cut 2

(fold)

BACK cut 1

GRAIN

Centre back (fold)

GRAIN

Ease between arrows

Shoulder

SLEEVE cut 2

GRAIN

SLEEVE
PLACKET
cut 2

Slit here

Pleat   Pleat

Boy's shirt and trousers cont.

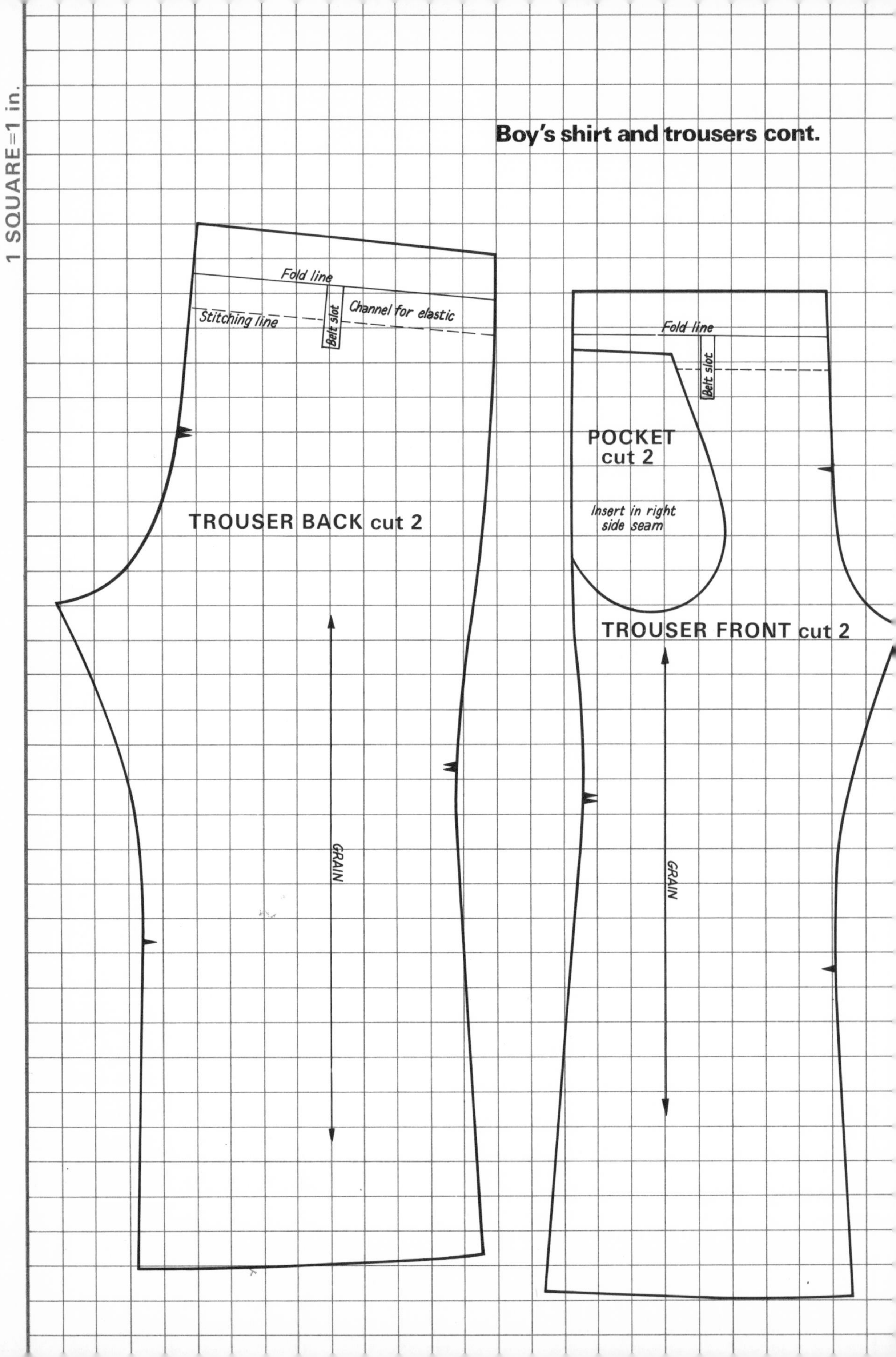
1 SQUARE=1 in.
Fold line
Channel for elastic
Stitching line
Belt slot
TROUSER BACK cut 2
GRAIN
Fold line
Belt slot
POCKET
cut 2
Insert in right
side seam
TROUSER FRONT cut 2
GRAIN

Tunic and trousers-
for a teenager

illustrated in colour on page 89

MATERIALS

For tunic: $\frac{7}{8}$yd. of fabric, 68in. wide; 8 eyelets; 1yd. of silk cord.
For trousers: $1\frac{3}{8}$yd. of fabric, 68in. wide, or $2\frac{1}{2}$yd. of fabric, 36in. wide; a 7-in. trouser zipper; $\frac{3}{4}$yd. of shaped waist petersham ribbon, $\frac{5}{8}$in. wide; 1 hook and eye.

FABRIC SUGGESTIONS

Our tunic and trousers are made up in wear-dated Acrilan jersey by Epatra, the tunic is in a red and blue patterned fabric, the trousers in co-ordinating plain red.

SIZE NOTE

The pattern as given will comfortably fit a teenage size 10 (bust size 32in., hip size 34in.). To adapt the pattern to fit a larger or smaller size, see page 106.

TO MAKE YOUR PATTERN

The diagrams on pages 133—4 gives the pieces you need. One square on the diagram equals 1in. Prepare your full-size pattern on squared paper, following instructions on page 106. Cut out fabric, following cutting-out layouts on page 132. As tunic is cut from single thickness fabric, it will be necessary to cut sleeve and neck facing sections twice (remember to reverse the pattern for second cutting) and to cut round outer edges of tunic back, front and front facing sections, then unpin and reverse pattern pieces to give remainder of complete pattern piece, pin in place and cut out.
Cut pocket facing from single thickness trouser fabric, and also from trouser fabric cut a strip 8in. by $3\frac{1}{2}$in. for zipper placket.
Unless otherwise stated, all seams should be stitched $\frac{5}{8}$in. from the edge of fabric; press all seams open after stitching.

TO MAKE
Tunic

Cut slit in centre front of tunic front, and front facing, as marked on pattern. Stay-stitch close to slit on both pieces.
Right sides together stitch tunic front to tunic back at shoulders and side seams.
Right sides together, stitch front facing to back neck facing at shoulder seams.
Right sides together, pin entire facing section to tunic, lining up neck edges and matching shoulder seams. Stitch, tapering stitching almost to nothing at point of centre front slit. Layer seams and clip carefully. Turn facing to wrong side. Neaten outer edges and catch to inside of tunic at shoulder seams with a few neat stitches. Make eyelets on either side of front opening, as marked on pattern.

Detail of lace-up eyelet fastening on tunic.

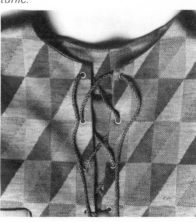

Right sides together, stitch underarm seam in each sleeve. Fold lower edge to wrong side on fold line marked, and stitch neatly. Set sleeves into armholes, matching notches, and easing head of sleeve to fit armhole as marked.

Turn up hem at lower edge to length required, and stitch. Thread cord through eyelet holes to fasten.

Make patch pocket, as described on page 42, and facing it with a strip of trouser fabric. Sew to tunic in position indicated.

Trousers

Stitch darts in trousers front and back, as indicated by guide lines on pattern. Right sides together stitch trousers back at centre back edges, and stitch trouser front at centre front edges, leaving seam open from waist down as marked for zipper. Fold back underlap on right front to wrong side, then stitch zipper in place, following instructions on page 57 for inserting a fly-front zipper in trousers, and catching in placket strip with left front seam: fold placket strip in half lengthwise, wrong sides together, then when zipper is basted to left front, place placket under zip, so its raw edges line up with folded-back seam allowance on left front edge, and fold extends towards centre front to form an underlap of about 1in. Stitch close to zipper teeth through all thicknesses. Right sides together, stitch trousers front to back down side edges.

Right sides together, stitch inner leg seams.

Place petersham ribbon to right side of trousers round waist edge, and stitch. Turn to wrong side, turn in ends of ribbon, trimming away any excess, and slip-stitch neatly to edge of centre front opening.

Turn up hem at lower edge of ·each trouser leg to length required, and stitch.

Sew hook and eye to fasten waist edge above zipper.

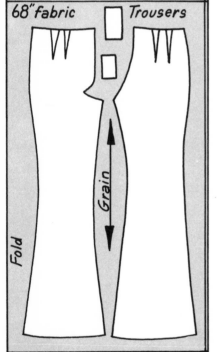

Cutting-out layouts

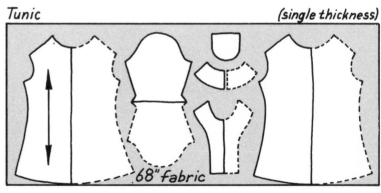

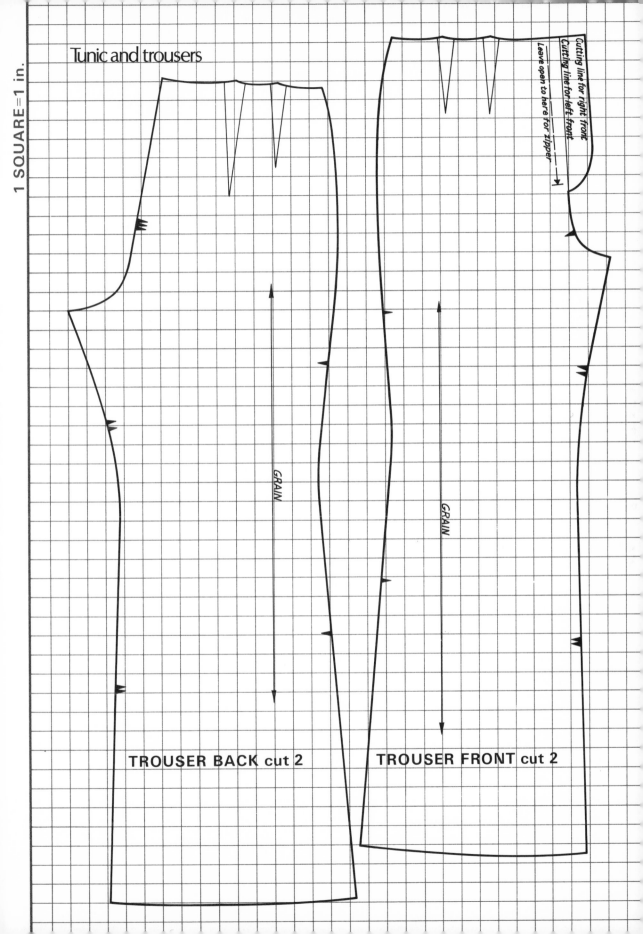

1 SQUARE=1 in.

Tunic and trousers

Cutting line for right front
Cutting line for left front
Leave open to here for zipper

GRAIN

GRAIN

TROUSER BACK cut 2

TROUSER FRONT cut 2

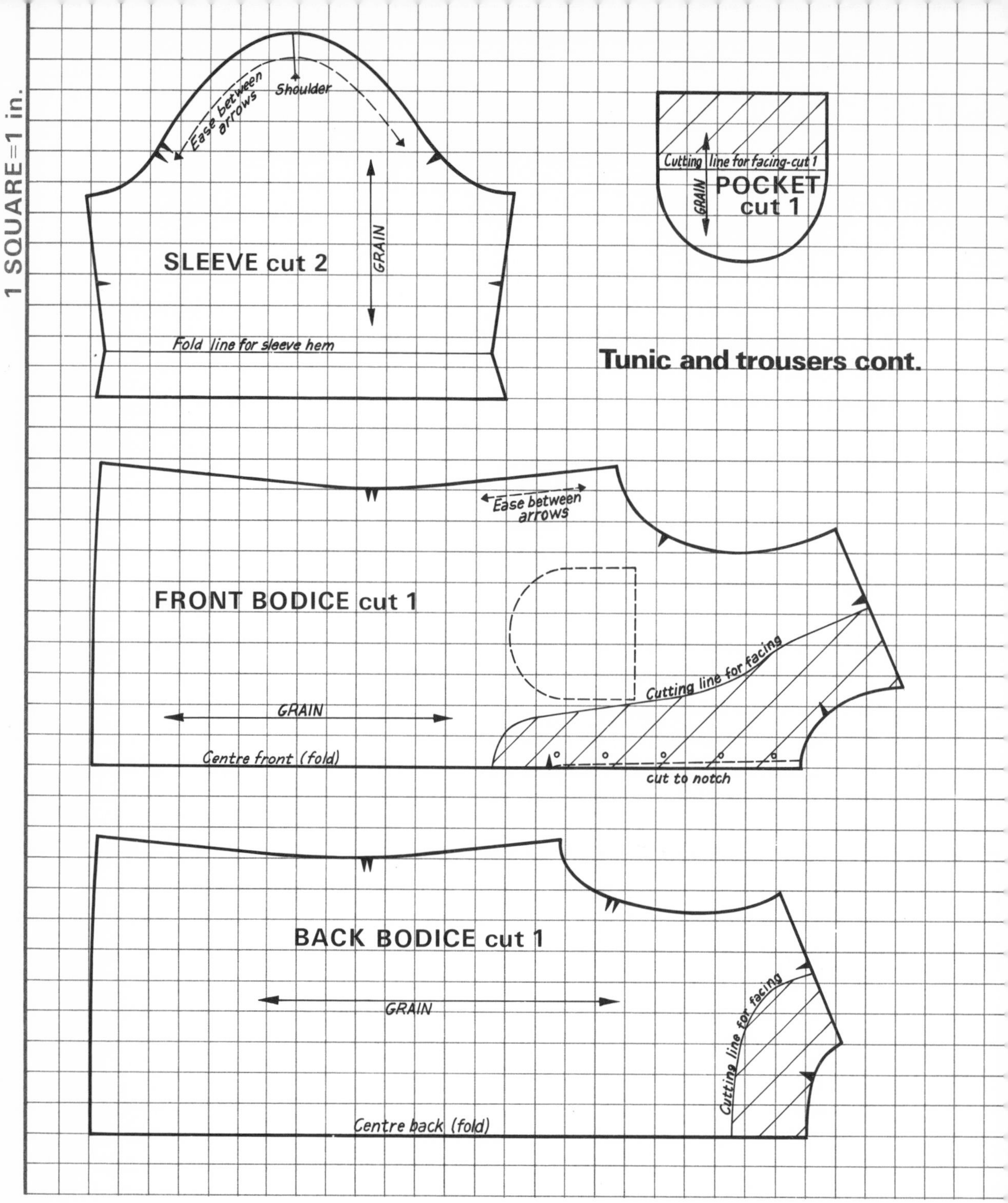
1 SQUARE=1 in.
Shoulder
Ease between arrows
SLEEVE cut 2
GRAIN
Fold line for sleeve hem
Cutting line for facing-cut 1
POCKET cut 1
GRAIN
Tunic and trousers cont.
Ease between arrows
FRONT BODICE cut 1
Cutting line for facing
GRAIN
Centre front (fold)
cut to notch
BACK BODICE cut 1
GRAIN
Cutting line for facing
Centre back (fold)

Safari jacket

illustrated in colour on page 89

MATERIALS

$2\frac{7}{8}$yd. of fabric, 36in. wide, or $2\frac{3}{8}$yd. of fabric, 45in. wide; eleven $\frac{5}{8}$-in. buttons; a $1\frac{1}{2}$-in. buckle; 5 eyelets.

FABRIC SUGGESTION

Our jacket is made up in a polyester and cotton gaberdine.

SIZE NOTE

The pattern as given will comfortably fit a teenager size 10 (bust size 32in., hip size 34in.). To adapt the pattern to fit a bigger or smaller size, see page 106.

TO MAKE YOUR PATTERN

The diagram on pages 137–8 gives the pieces you need. One square on the diagram equals 1in. Prepare your full-size pattern on squared paper, following instructions on page 106. Cut out fabric following cutting-out layouts on page 136. Place jacket back on fold of fabric, as indicated, to avoid a seam at this point in he garment. Cut 2 strips, each $3\frac{1}{2}$ by $1\frac{1}{2}$in., for belt carriers.

Unless otherwise stated, all seams should be stitched $\frac{5}{8}$in. from the edge of fabric; press all seams open after stitching.

TO MAKE

Stitch back shoulder darts as indicated by guide lines on the pattern.

On jacket front sections, fold back facings on to right side on fold line marked on pattern. Stitch from fold at neck edge as far as centre front. Trim and clip seam, turn facings to wrong side and press well. Neaten long edges of facings.

Make up four patch pockets (two top pockets, two lower pockets), following instructions on page 42, and stitch to jacket fronts in positions marked on pattern.

Make each pocket flap as follows: place pair of flap sections together, right sides facing, and stitch down both short sides, and the long shaped side (leave long straight side unstitched). Layer and clip seam and turn pocket flap right side out. Press well. Fold back raw edges along straight edge, and baste. Make a hand-worked buttonhole on flap, as marked on pattern. Stitch flaps in position above pockets as marked on pattern pieces. Using a flat-felled seam join jacket back to fronts at shoulder and side seams.

Place collar sections right sides together, and stitch round outer edges (leave neck edges unstitched). Layer and clip seam, and turn right side out. Press.

Pin collar in position to right side of jacket. Fold back front facings on top of collar, lining up neck edges. Stitch neck seam,

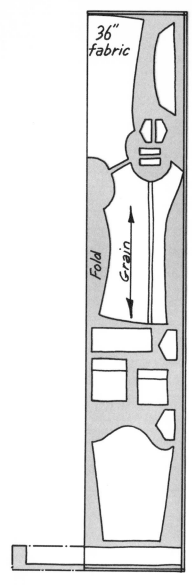

36"
fabric

Fold

Grain

Safari Jacket

stitching through all fabric thicknesses at front of jacket as far as shoulder seams, and then stitching through jacket fabric and under collar only at the back neck edge. Layer and clip seam, and turn facings to wrong side of jacket. Turn in seam allowance on top collar edge at back neck and slip-stitch neatly by hand to inside of back neck edge seam just stitched. Turn in seam allowance at shoulder edge of facings, and slip-stitch to inside of jacket shoulder seam.

On right front make five hand-worked buttonholes at positions marked on pattern.

Using a flat-felled seam, stitch long seam in each sleeve, leaving lower edge open as marked. Turn in and stitch raw edges on this opening, tapering seam allowance to nothing at top of opening. Pleat lower edge of sleeve, as marked on pattern. Baste to hold pleats in position.

Fold each cuff section in half, right sides together.

Stitch down each short edge and along the long edge as far as solid line marking on pattern (this is the end opposite button-hole end). Layer and clip seam. Turn right side out. Work buttonhole in position marked.

Pin cuff to right side of sleeve lower edge, matching notch marking, and letting stitched end of cuff form an underlap under buttonhole.

Stitch cuff seam, stitching only through sleeve fabric and a single thickness of cuff. Press seam down towards cuff. Turn in seam allowance on remaining edge of cuff, and slip-stitch neatly by hand to inside of cuff seam just stitched.

Set sleeves into jacket, matching notches, underarm and shoulder markings. Use a flat-felled seam.

Open out front facings, and turn up and stitch a narrow hem round lower edge of jacket. Fold back facings and slip-stitch to hem at lower edge.

Sew buttons to left front, to cuffs, and to each pocket to correspond with buttonholes worked.

Work top-stitching if wished round collar, cuff and pocket edges. To make belt, fold belt strip in half lengthwise, right sides together, and stitch short edges and long edge, leaving a gap in the seam. Turn right side out, turn in seam allowance on gap, and slip-stitch closed. Press belt well, and run a row of top-stitching right round edge. Stitch straight end over bar of buckle. Make five eyelets near other end. To make each belt carrier, fold fabric strip in half lengthwise, wrong sides together. Turn in raw edges and stitch. Press well, then run a row of top-stitching down the length of strip at each side. Turn in short edges and stitch in position to right side of jacket.

Cutting-out layouts

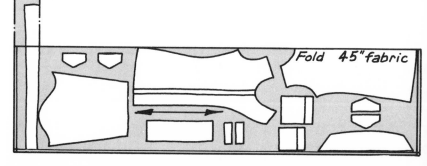

Fold 45" fabric

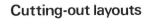

1 SQUARE = 1 in.

Safari jacket

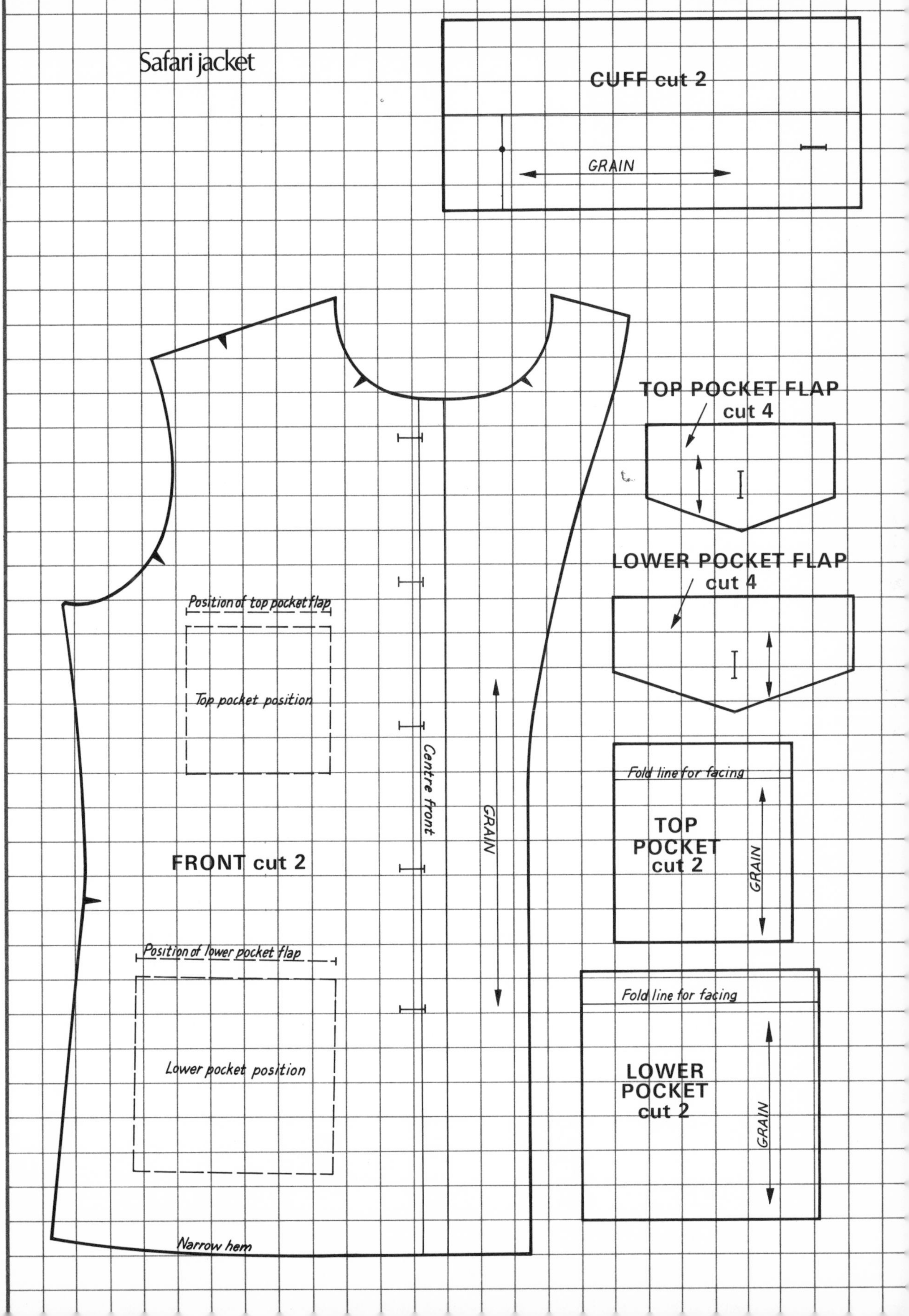

CUFF cut 2

GRAIN

TOP POCKET FLAP
cut 4

LOWER POCKET FLAP
cut 4

Position of top pocket flap

Top pocket position

Fold line for facing

TOP POCKET cut 2

GRAIN

FRONT cut 2

Centre front

GRAIN

Position of lower pocket flap

Lower pocket position

Fold line for facing

LOWER POCKET cut 2

GRAIN

Narrow hem

Safari jacket cont.

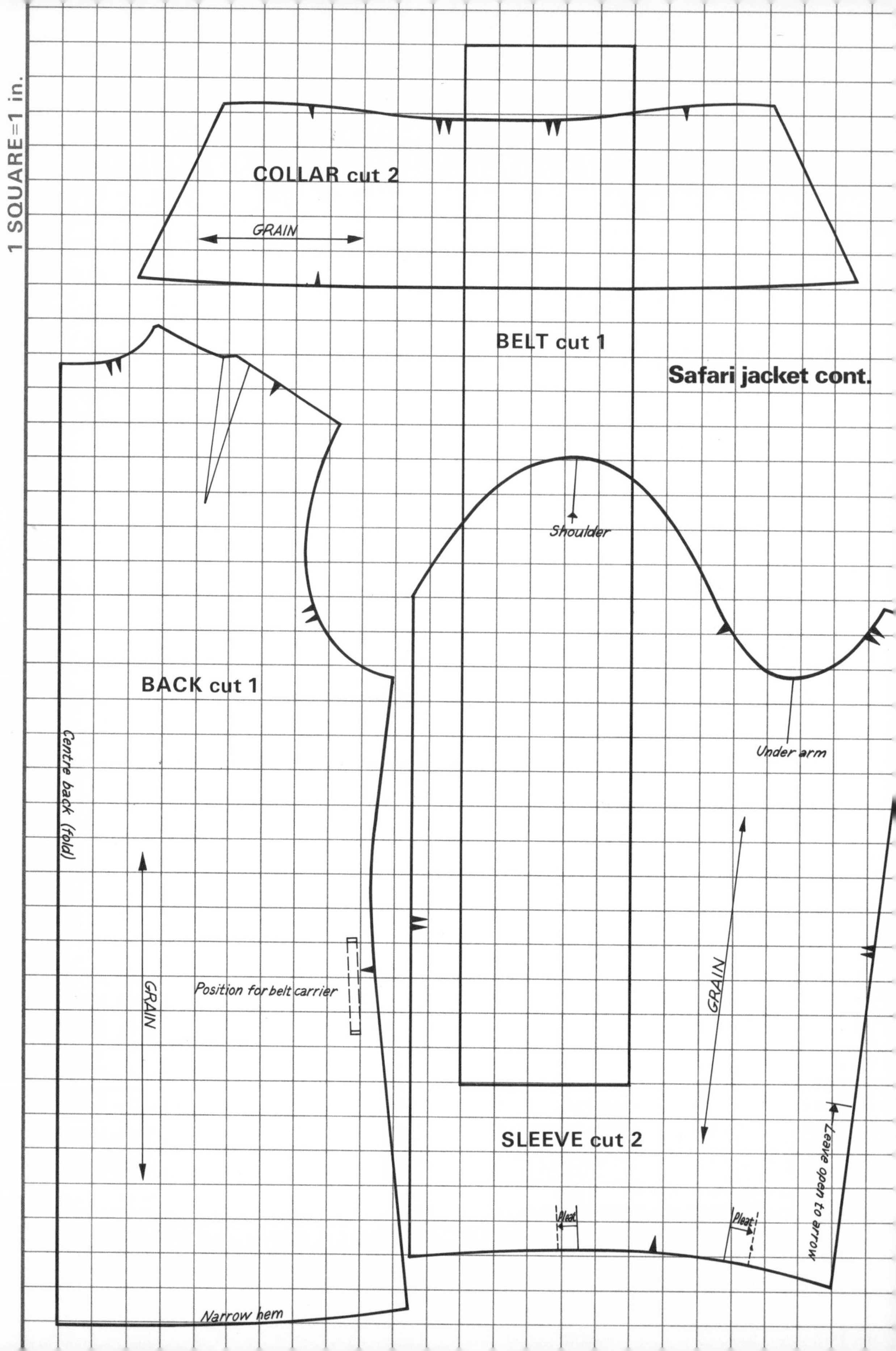
1 SQUARE=1 in.
COLLAR cut 2
GRAIN
BELT cut 1
Shoulder
BACK cut 1
Centre back (fold)
GRAIN
Position for belt carrier
Narrow hem
Under arm
GRAIN
SLEEVE cut 2
Leave open to arrow
Pleat
Pleat

Mother and daughter
beach dresses- *with matching bikini pants*

illustrated in colour on page 143

MATERIALS

For mother's dress and pants : 2¾yd. of fabric, 36in. wide, or 2⅜yd. of fabric, 45in. wide; 1½yd. narrow elastic; 3yd. ric-rac braid trimming in a colour to match or contrast with fabric colour; three ¾-in. buttons (alternatively, if it is not wished to make buttonholes then a strip of self-adhesive fastening can be used—you will need a strip of about 6in.). **For daughter's dress and pants :** 1⅞yd. of fabric, 36in. wide, or 1⅜yd. of fabric, 45in. wide; 1yd. narrow elastic; 2½yd. ric-rac briad trimming in a colour to match or contrast with fabric colour; two ¾-in. buttons (alternatively, if it is not wished to make buttonholes then a strip of self-adhesive fastening can be used—you will need a strip of about 4½in.).

FABRIC SUGGESTION

Our dresses are made in a cotton seersucker, orange with a white spot pattern, and trimmed with white ric-rac braid.

SIZE NOTE

The pattern as given will comfortably fit bust size 34in. and hip size 36in. (for mother's dress), and a girl of about six years old, with a chest measurement of 24in. (for child's dress). Centre back length: 22in. (mother's dress), 15½in. (daughter's dress). To adapt the pattern to fit a bigger or smaller size, see page 106.

TO MAKE YOUR PATTERN

The diagram on pages 141–2 gives the pieces you need. One square on the diagram equals 1in. Prepare your full-size pattern on squared paper, following instructions on page 106. Cut out fabric, following cutting-out layouts on pages 140 and 142. Place skirt front section on fold of fabric, as indicated, to avoid a seam at these points in the garment. Pants back and front sections should also be cut on the fold to avoid seams at centre back and front. It will be necessary to cut these pieces from single thickness fabric: pin pattern piece as indicated, cut round outer edges, then unpin and carefully reverse the pattern piece to give remainder of whole piece, pin and cut out. Strap sections will also have to be cut in this way for daughter's dress cut from 36-in. fabric.

Unless otherwise stated, all seams should be stitched ⅝in. from the edge of fabric; press all seams open after stitching.

TO MAKE
Mother's dress and pants

Dress. Two of the bodice sections will be used for the right side of dress; the other two sections will form a lining and facing in one. Work with right-side sections first: stitch darts, by bringing

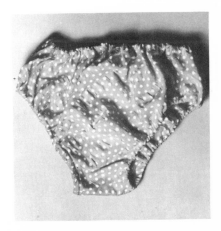

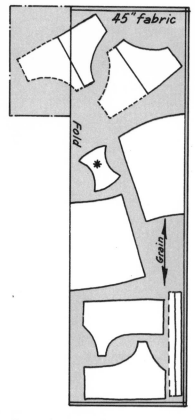

45" fabric

Fold

Grain

Daughter's Dress

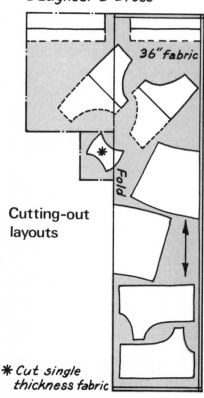

36" fabric

Fold

Cutting-out layouts

* Cut single thickness fabric

dotted line markings together. Clip into 'V' point of dart, and press dart open. Right sides together, stitch bodice sections together at centre front seam.

Fold each strap section in half lengthwise, right sides together. Stitch across one short edge and down long seam. Turn right side out. Pin each strap to bodice front top edge, on right side, lining up raw edges (so strap hangs down towards waist edge). Baste.

Stitch darts and centre front seam in lining sections.

Now place lining to main bodice section, right sides together (straps will now be sandwiched between the two layers of bodice fabric). Line up outer edges carefully, and pin in place. Stitch right round all outer edges except waist edge (leave this open). Layer and clip seam as necessary, and turn lining to inside. Press well.

Baste waist edges together.

Right sides together, stitch skirt front to backs at side seams. Right sides together, stitch skirt to bodice round waist edge, leaving section beyond fold line on skirt centre back free. Ease skirt to fit bodice as necessary. Match notches and side seam on skirt to side seam indication on bodice pattern piece. Stitch waist seam. Layer and clip seam. Turn in seam allowance on centre back extensions, then fold to wrong side along fold line marked on pattern, to form a facing. Slip-stitch neatly by hand to inside of waist seam already stitched. Make narrow hem along lower edge, opening out facings to stitch hem. Fold facings back in position and slip-stitch to hem along lower edge. Make buttonholes in right back of bodice section, as marked on pattern, and stitch buttons to left back to correspond. Alternatively stitch strip of self-adhesive fastening to these edges.

Stitch ric-rac braid to bodice, starting at centre back waist, and bringing right round waist edge to centre front, then up centre front and round top edges of bodice to finish at centre back top edge. Repeat with other half of bodice.

Pants. Right sides together, stitch pants back to pants front at side seams, and at crutch. On inside of pants, lay gusset in position, wrong sides together; turn in raw edges on gusset, then edge-stitch neatly to pants.

Turn in and stitch narrow hem round waist and leg edges as marked on pattern. Leave a gap in each seam, and thread through elastic to fit. Stitch elastic ends together, and slip-stitch seams closed.

Daughter's dress and pants

Make as for mother's dress, but instead of stitching darts in dress bodice, make small pleat as indicated on pattern piece, by folding on solid line and pleating to broken line.

Run two rows of gathering stitching round waist edge of skirt, pull up gathers and adjust to fit waist edge of bodice, matching notches and side seams as before.

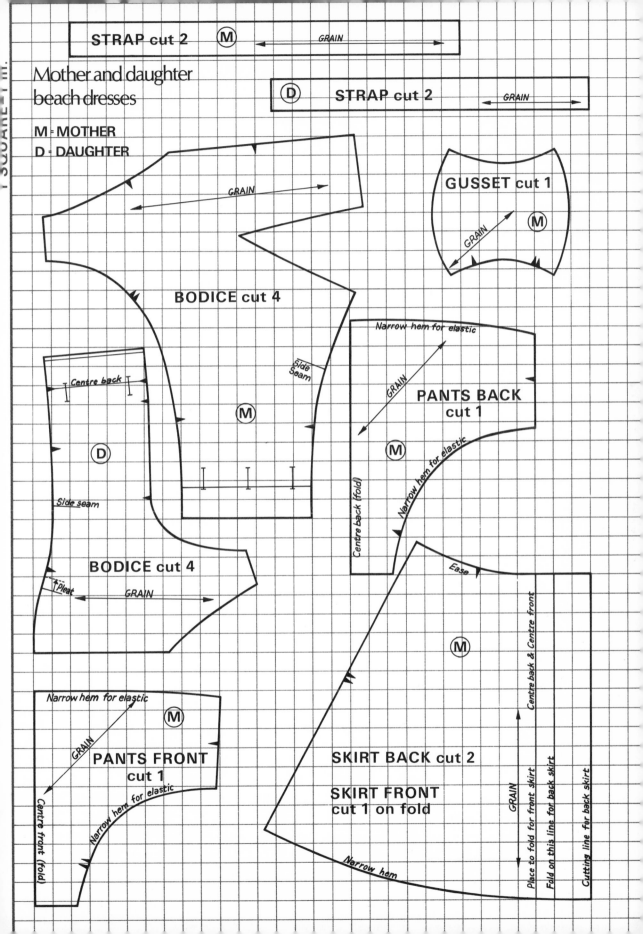

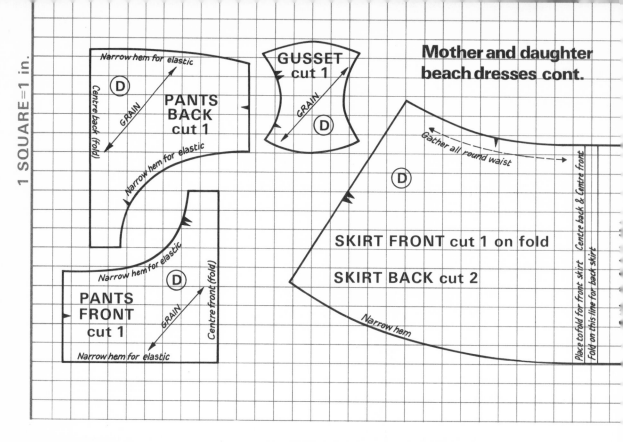

1 SQUARE = 1 in.

PANTS BACK cut 1

D

Narrow hem for elastic

Centre back (fold)

GRAIN

Narrow hem for elastic

GUSSET cut 1

D

GRAIN

PANTS FRONT cut 1

D

Narrow hem for elastic

Centre front (fold)

GRAIN

Narrow hem for elastic

Gather all round waist

D

SKIRT FRONT cut 1 on fold

SKIRT BACK cut 2

Narrow hem

Place to fold for front skirt

Centre back & Centre front

Fold on this line for back skirt

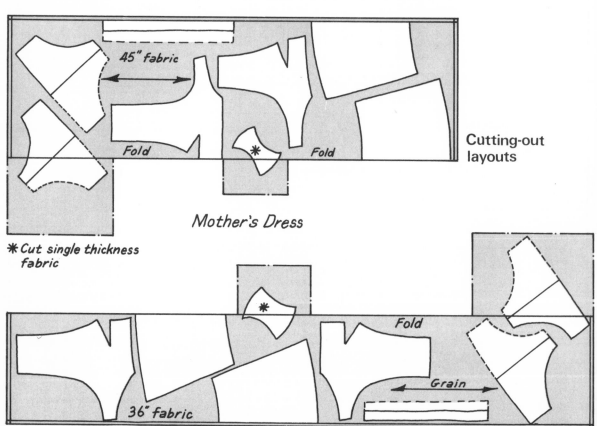

Cutting-out layouts

45" fabric

Fold

Fold

Mother's Dress

Cut single thickness fabric

*

36" fabric

Fold

Grain

142

Man's two-way shirt: sports version with short sleeves and open neck above, and long-sleeved, high-collared version (right)

Man's shirt

Two versions from the same pattern—long-sleeved shirt has a high neck fastening, short-sleeved, sports shirt has an open neck and interfaced front edges.

MATERIALS
For long-sleeved shirt: 3yd. of fabric, 36in. wide, or 2½yd. of fabric, 45in. wide; ¼yd. of interfacing, 32 or 36in. wide; eight ½-in. buttons. **For sports shirt:** 2¾yd. of fabric, 36in. wide, or 2yd. of fabric, 45in. wide; ½yd. of interfacing, 32 or 36in. wide; five ½-in. buttons.

FABRIC SUGGESTIONS
Our long-sleeved shirt is made up in a polyester crêpe; the sports shirt is made up in Swiss cotton voile.

SIZE NOTE
The pattern as given will comfortably fit chest size 40in., neck size 15½in. To adapt the pattern to fit a bigger or smaller size, see page 106.

TO MAKE YOUR PATTERN
The diagram on pages 149 and 149 gives the pattern pieces you need. One square equals 1in. Prepare your full-size pattern on squared paper, following instructions on page 106. Cut out fabric, following cutting-out layouts on pages 146–7. Shirt back should be placed on fold of fabric, as indicated, to avoid a seam at this point in the garment. Collar for sports shirt should similarly be placed on fold of fabric.
From single thickness interfacing, cut 1 collar section and 2 cuffs (half width of cuff pattern only), for long-sleeved shirt; cut 2 front facing sections and half the collar section (fold pattern in half lengthwise) for sports shirt.
Unless otherwise stated, all seams should be stitched ⅝in. from the edge of fabric; press all seams open after stitching.

TO MAKE
Long-sleeved shirt
Pin one yoke section to back shirt, right sides together, lining up straight edge of yoke section with top edge of shirt back. Baste. Now on the wrong side of shirt back, pin other yoke section, right side of yoke against wrong side of shirt back and lining up straight edges as before. Baste, then stitch along edge, through all three layers of fabric. Layer and clip seam, and fold yoke sections up so their wrong sides are together and second yoke section acts as a facing for the first. Baste together round armhole edges.
Now with right side of inside yoke against wrong side of shirt

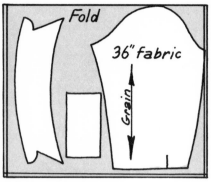

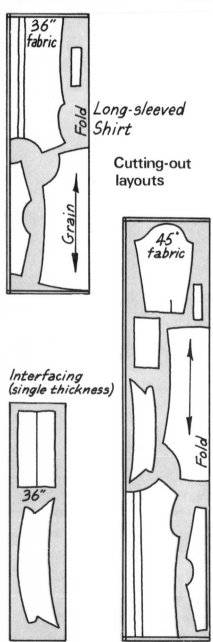

Long-sleeved Shirt

Cutting-out layouts

Interfacing
(single thickness)

front, stitch inside yoke to shirt front at shoulders. Press seams up. Turn in seam allowance along shoulder edges of top yoke, pin in place over seams just stitched (right side of shirt), and edge-stitch through all three thicknesses of material.

Baste neck edges of yokes together.

Iron on or baste on interfacing to wrong side of one collar section (this will be the top collar). Pin top collar and undercollar together right sides facing, and stitch round outer edges (leave neck edges unstitched). Layer and clip seam, clipping into corner sections as marked, and turn right side out, taking care to get good sharp points at the corners. Pin collar to right side of neck edge of shirt, so undercollar is facing right side of shirt. Line up neck edges, and match centre front points. Stitch, stitching only through shirt fabric and undercollar only. Layer and clip seam. Turn in seam allowance on remaining edge on top collar and slip-stitch neatly by hand to inside of neck edge seam just stitched. Neaten outer edges of shirt front facing sections, then fold to wrong side on fold line marked on pattern. Turn in seam allowance at neck edge, and slip-stitch neatly to inside of collar neck edge.

Make worked buttonholes in left front of shirt, as marked on pattern pieces—the top buttonhole which is in the collar section is a horizontal one; the remainder, on left front, are all vertical. Sew sleeves into armholes of shirt, matching notches and easing head of sleeves to fit armholes between arrows as marked. Use a flat-felled seam or a French seam.

Now, using either a flat-felled or French seam, stitch each side seam and underarm seam in one long continuous seam. Begin stitching at lower edge of side seam so you are sewing towards and into the 'tube' of the sleeve.

At lower edge of each sleeve work a 'V' of stitching as marked on pattern piece, slit between stitching almost as far as tip of 'V'. Make a narrow hem along edge of 'V' nearest to underarm seam; face the other edge with placket strip: to do this, fold placket strip in half lengthwise and stitch across one short end and down long edge for $\frac{5}{8}$in. Trim and clip seam and turn right side out. Press well.

Right sides together, pin placket strip to sleeve opening, having stitched section of placket at tip of 'V', and lining up raw edges at lower edges of sleeve. Stitch, taking stitching through sleeve fabric and one layer of placket fabric only. Clip seam, turn in seam allowance on remaining long open edge of placket and slip-stitch neatly by hand to wrong side of seam just stitched. Make pleat on lower edge of sleeve. Baste in place.

Fold one cuff section together lengthwise, right sides facing. Iron on or baste on interfacing to one side. Stitch side seams. Trim seams, and turn cuff right side out. Make worked buttonhole in cuff, as marked on pattern.

Right sides together, pin cuff to lower edge of one sleeve, lining up edges, and having buttonhole at the faced end of opening. Stitch, taking stitching through sleeve fabric and one layer of cuff only. Layer and clip seam. Turn in seam allowance on remaining edge of cuff, and slip-stitch neatly by hand to inside of cuff seam. Stitch other cuff to other sleeve in a similar way. Open out front facings, and make a narrow hem along lower edge of shirt; stitch. Fold back front facings and slip-stitch to hem along lower edge. Sew on buttons to correspond with all buttonholes. Work top-stitching round collar and cuffs.

Sports shirt

Iron on or baste on interfacing to wrong side of each shirt front facing section. Neaten outer edges of facings. Fold facings to right side along fold line marked, and stitch from fold at neck edge to centre front point. Trim and clip seams, and turn right side out. Press well. Stitch yoke sections, and back and front of shirt together, as for long-sleeved shirt.

Fold collar section in half lengthwise, right sides together, and iron on or baste on interfacing to one side. Stitch short side edges of collar. Trim and clip seam, and turn collar right side out, taking care to get good sharp points at the corners. Pin collar to neck edge of shirt, so layer of collar without interfacing (undercollar) is facing right side of shirt. Keep shirt front facings clear until collar is pinned in place, then turn facings inside out, and lining up neck edges, pin interfacings in place so right side of facings are against top collar. Stitch, stitching through all layers of fabric from centre front points as far as shoulder seams, and then stitching only through shirt fabric and undercollar only. Layer and clip seam, and turn facings to wrong side of shirt. Turn in seam allowance on back neck edge of top collar, and slip-stitch neatly by hand to wrong side of neck edge seam just stitched.

Turn in seam allowance on shoulder edges of front facings and slip-stitch to inside of shoulder seams.

Make worked buttonholes in left front, as marked on pattern. Using a flat-felled seam, stitch underarm seam in each sleeve. Turn in hem at lower edge of sleeve as marked on pattern, and stitch neatly. Set sleeves into armholes, matching notches, and easing sleeves to fit armholes as marked. Use a flat-felled seam. Open out front facings and make a narrow hem along lower edge. Fold back facings, and slip-stitch to hem along lower edge. Sew on buttons to correspond with buttonholes.

Make patch pocket, as described on page 42, and stitch to shirt left front in position indicated.

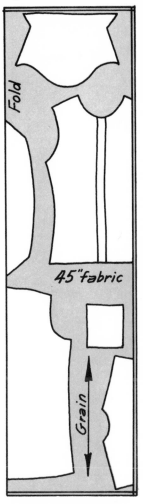

45" fabric

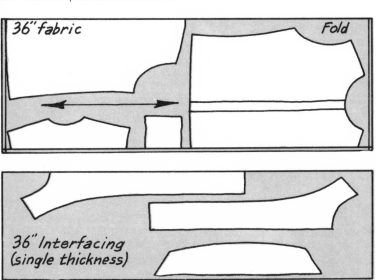

36" fabric

36" Interfacing (single thickness)

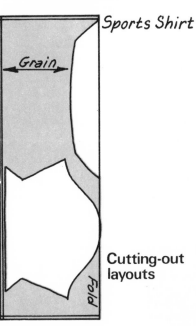

Sports Shirt

Cutting-out layouts

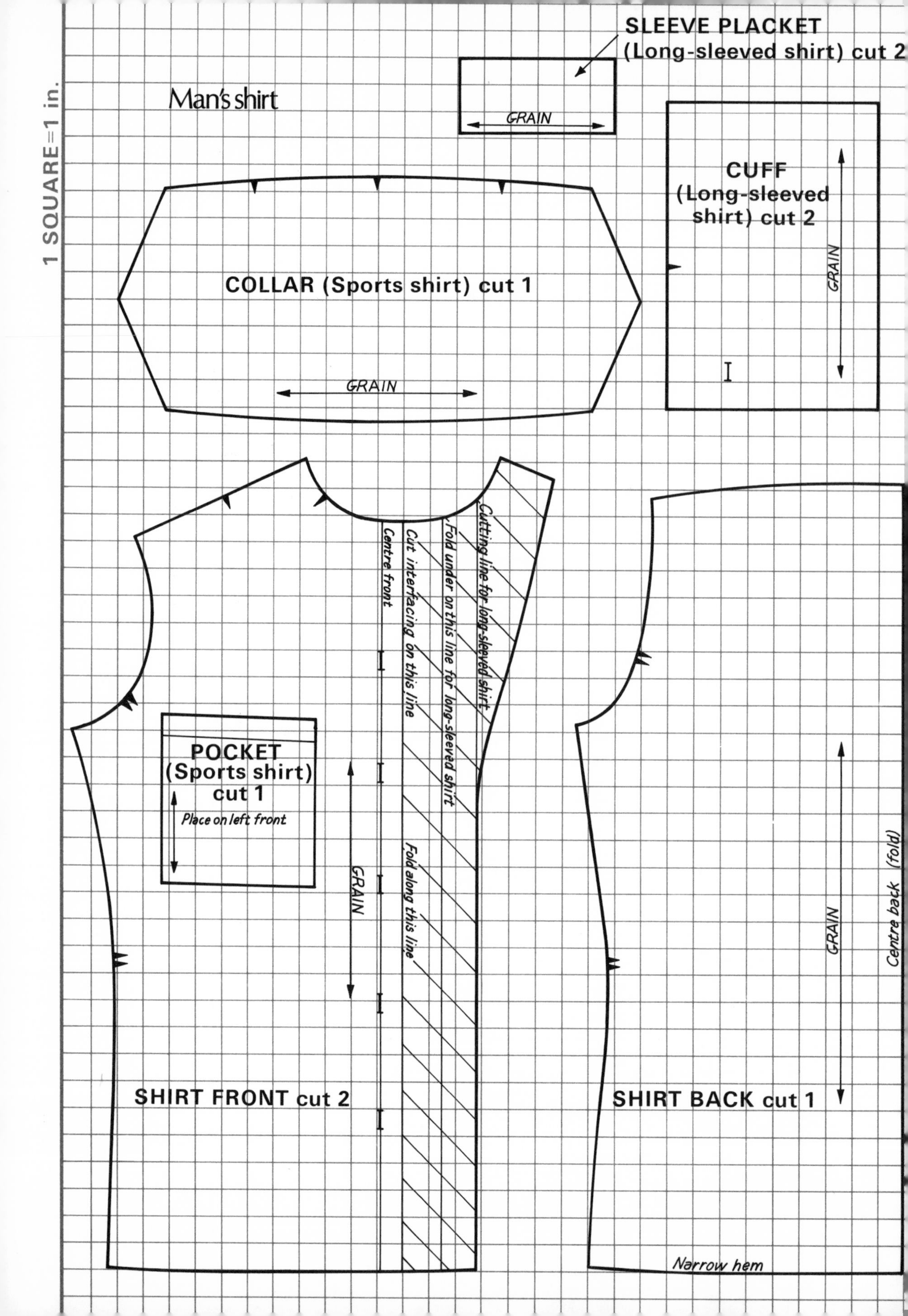

1 SQUARE=1 in.

Man's shirt

SLEEVE PLACKET
(Long-sleeved shirt) cut 2

GRAIN

CUFF
(Long-sleeved
shirt) cut 2

GRAIN

COLLAR (Sports shirt) cut 1

GRAIN

Cutting line for long-sleeved shirt

Fold under on this line for long-sleeved shirt

Cut interfacing on this line

Centre front

Fold along this line

POCKET
(Sports shirt)
cut 1

Place on left front

GRAIN

GRAIN

Centre back (fold)

SHIRT FRONT cut 2

SHIRT BACK cut 1

Narrow hem

1 SQUARE = 1 in.

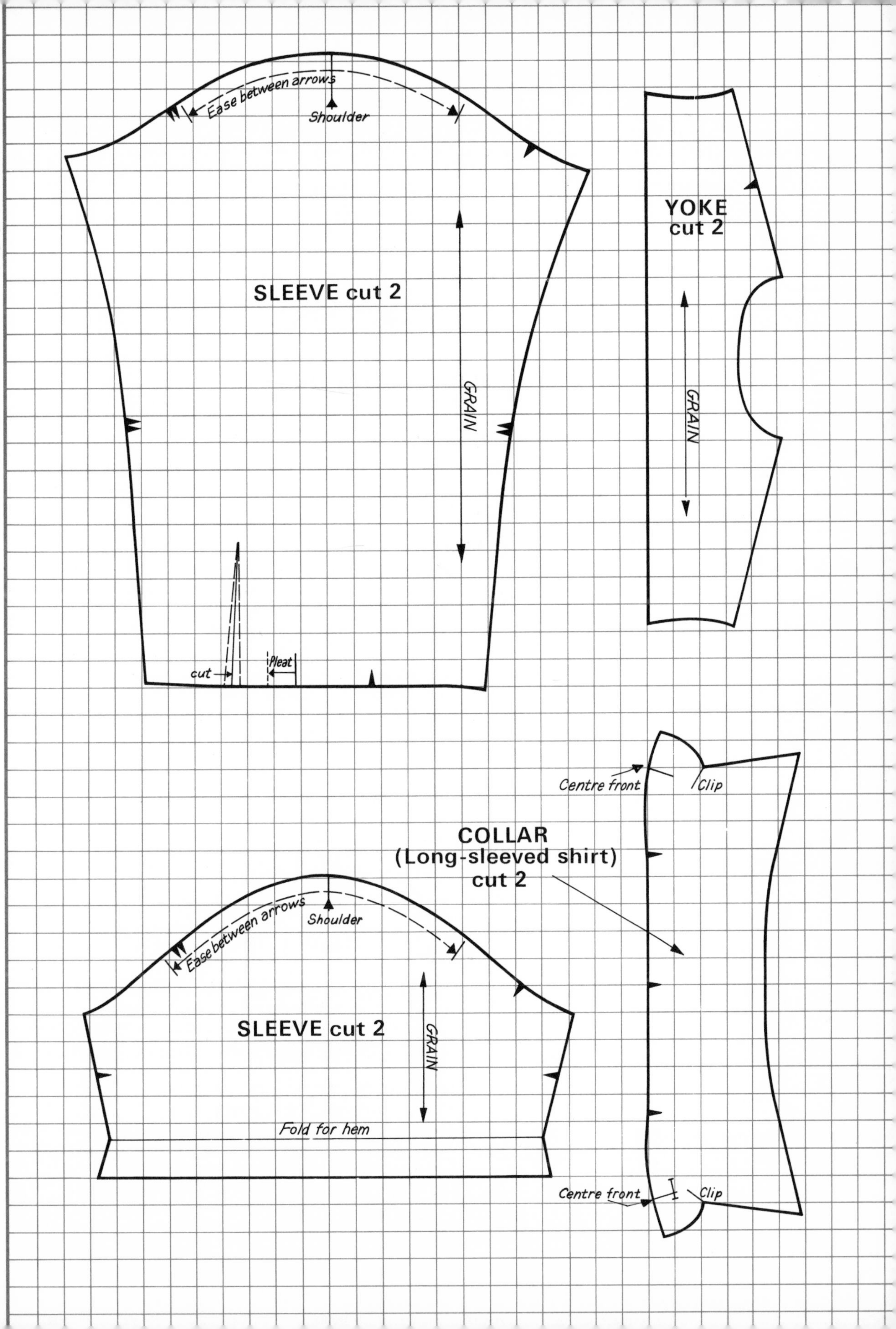

SLEEVE cut 2

Ease between arrows

Shoulder

GRAIN

cut →

Pleat

YOKE cut 2

GRAIN

Centre front

Clip

COLLAR (Long-sleeved shirt) cut 2

SLEEVE cut 2

Ease between arrows

Shoulder

GRAIN

Fold for hem

Centre front

Clip

Smock dress

illustrated in colour on page 54

MATERIALS

$1\frac{3}{4}$yd. of fabric, 58in. wide, or $2\frac{1}{8}$yd. of fabric, 45in. wide; $\frac{3}{8}$yd. of fabric, 36in. wide, for tie; $\frac{1}{4}$yd. of interfacing, 32 or 36in. wide; a 16-in. zipper.

FABRIC SUGGESTION

Our dress is made up in a striped Courtelle by Epatra.

SIZE NOTE

The pattern as given will comfortably fit bust size 34in., hip size 36in. To adapt the pattern to fit a bigger or smaller size, see page 106.

TO MAKE YOUR PATTERN

The diagram on pages 152—3 gives the pieces you need. One square on the diagram equals 1in. Prepare your full-size pattern on squared paper, following instructions on page 106. Cut out fabric, following cutting-out layouts opposite. Back bodice and back skirt should both be placed on fold of fabric to avoid a seam at these points in the garment. If you are using a striped fabric where the pattern pieces must be cut so the skirt sections have stripes running vertically, the bodice and sleeves have the stripes running horizontally, be sure to follow the correct cutting-out layout. Cut bodice front from single thickness fabric, cutting the piece twice, and remembering to reverse the pattern after the first cutting. Cut bodice back from under layer of fabric, folding the fabric first so centre back edge can be placed against the fold—make sure that the stripes are running horizontally. Cut collar section once from single thickness interfacing.

Unless otherwise stated, all seams should be stitched $\frac{5}{8}$in. from the edge of fabric; press all seams open after stitching.

TO MAKE

Stitch bust darts in bodice front, and back shoulder darts in bodice back, as indicated by guide lines on pattern.

Right sides together, stitch skirt front sections together at centre front seam, leaving seam open at the top for zipper, as indicated on pattern piece.

Right sides together, stitch skirt front to bodice fronts at waist edge, matching notches. Press seam up.

Stitch zipper into centre front opening.

Right sides together, stitch skirt back to bodice back at waist edges, matching notches. Press seam up.

Right sides together, stitch dress front to dress back at shoulders and at side seams.

Iron on or baste on interfacing to wrong side of one collar

section (this will be top collar). Right sides together, pin then stitch undercollar to collar round outer edges, leaving neck edge unstitched.

Layer and clip seam, and turn collar right side out, making sure you have good points at the corners.

Pin collar to neck edge of dress, so undercollar is facing right side of dress, and matching notches. Stitch, only stitching through dress fabric and undercollar. Layer and clip seam, turn in seam allowance along remaining edge of top collar, and slip-stitch neatly by hand on inside of neck edge seam just stitched.

On each sleeve stitch underarm sleeve, right sides together. Turn in cuff edge along fold line marked and hemstitch neatly in place. Set sleeves into armholes of dress, matching notches, and easing round head of each sleeve, as marked on pattern. Turn up lower hem of dress to length required, and stitch.

To make tie, cut out pattern shape from double thickness fabric, placing pattern on fold of fabric as indicated.

Fold tie in half lengthwise, and stitch right round open edges, leaving a gap in the seam to turn right side out. Turn right side out. Make a pleat as indicated on pattern and run a row of machine stitching across centre of pleat, at right angles to it. Stitch to centre back neck edge of dress, under collar at this point. Bring wide ends of tie to front of dress, bringing them under the collar, and make a single loose tie at the front.

Cutting-out layouts

Smock Dress

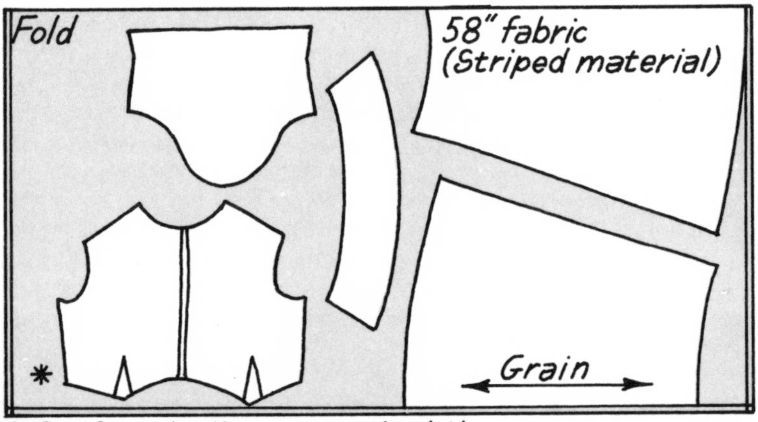

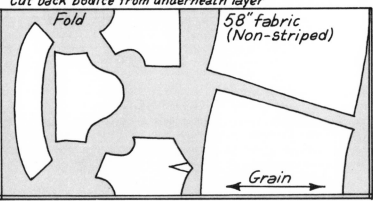

58" fabric (Striped material)

58" fabric (Non-striped)

* Cut front bodices on single cloth
  Cut back bodice from underneath layer

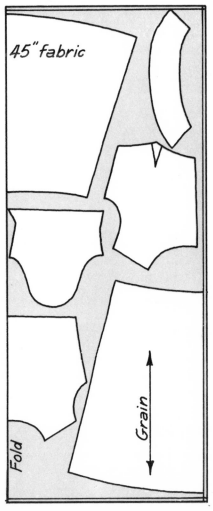

45" fabric

151

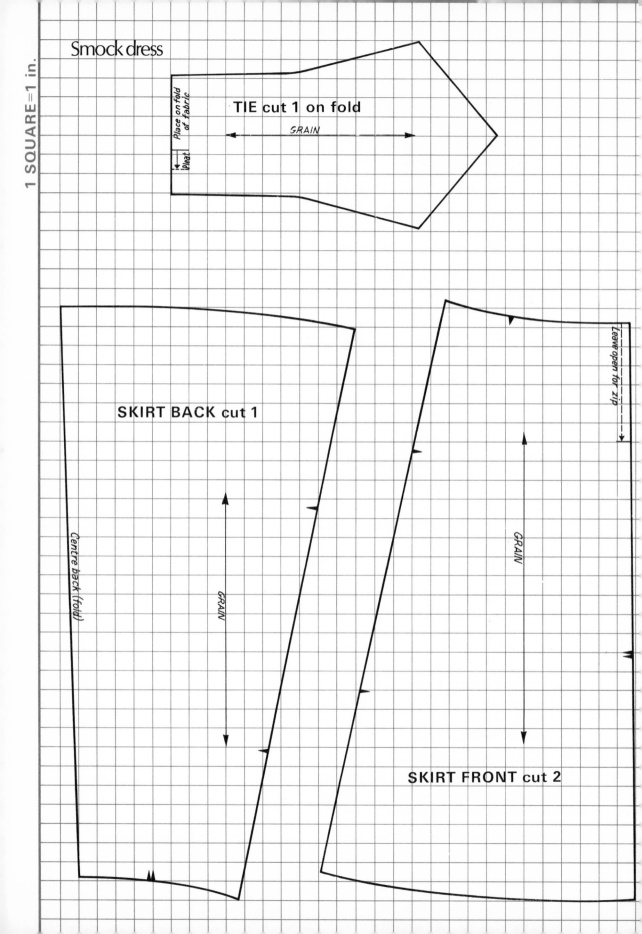

1 SQUARE=1 in.

Smock dress

TIE cut 1 on fold

Place on fold of fabric

Pleat

GRAIN

SKIRT BACK cut 1

Centre back (fold)

GRAIN

SKIRT FRONT cut 2

Leave open for zip

GRAIN

1 SQUARE=1 in.

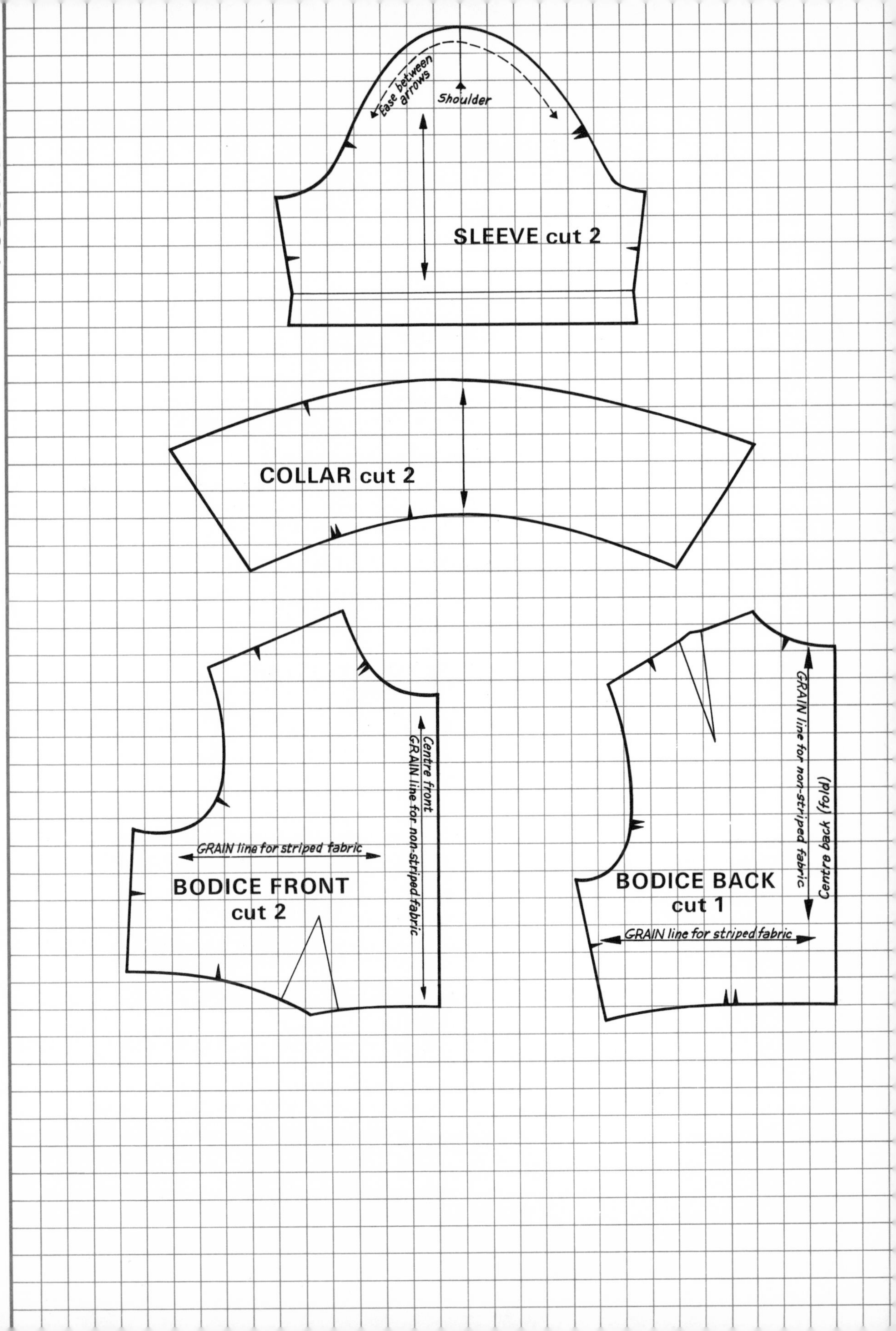

SLEEVE cut 2

Ease between arrows

Shoulder

COLLAR cut 2

BODICE FRONT cut 2

GRAIN line for striped fabric

Centre front
GRAIN line for non-striped fabric

BODICE BACK cut 1

GRAIN line for non-striped fabric

Centre back (fold)

GRAIN line for striped fabric

Two-way shift dress

illustrated in colour on page 71

A sleeveless, round-necked version for summer; a long-sleeved roll-collared version for winter.

MATERIALS
For sleeveless dress: $2\frac{5}{8}$yd. of fabric, 36in. wide, or $1\frac{3}{4}$yd. of fabric, 54in. wide; a 20-in. zipper; a $2\frac{1}{2}$-in. buckle. **For long-sleeved dress:** $2\frac{1}{8}$yd. of fabric, 54in. wide, or $3\frac{1}{2}$yd. of fabric, 36in. wide; a 20-in. zipper; 1 hook and eye.

FABRIC SUGGESTIONS
Our sleeveless dress is made in a printed pique cotton, in shades of blue with white, with a white buckle on the belt. The long-sleeved dress is made in a printed raschel jersey.

SIZE NOTE
The pattern as given will comfortably fit bust size 34in., hip size 36in. To adapt the pattern to fit a bigger or smaller size, see page 106.

TO MAKE YOUR PATTERN
The diagram on pages 156—7 gives the pieces you need. One square on the diagram equals 1in. Prepare your full-size pattern on squared paper, following instructions on page 106. Cut out fabric, following cutting-out layouts opposite. Dress front for long-sleeved dress, and dress front and front neck facing for sleeveless dress, all must be placed on fold of fabric. Belt for sleeveless dress must also be placed on fold of fabric.
Unless otherwise stated, all seams should be stitched $\frac{5}{8}$in. from the edge of fabric; press all seams open after stitching.

TO MAKE
Sleeveless dress
Stitch bust darts in dress front, and back shoulder darts in dress back, as indicated by guide lines on pattern.
Right sides together, stitch centre back seam, leaving seam open from neck edge down as marked on pattern. Stitch zipper into this opening.
Right sides together, stitch dress front to dress back at shoulders and side seams.
Right sides together, stitch front neck facing to back neck facings at shoulder seams.
Pin facing to neck edge of dress, right sides together, and matching notches and shoulder seams. Stitch right round neck edge. Layer and clip seam, and press facing to wrong side of dress. Turn in raw edges of facings at centre back opening and slip-stitch neatly to tapes of zipper. Neaten outer edge of facing, and catch facing to shoulder seams with a few neat stitches.

Right sides together, stitch one front armhole facing to one back armhole facing at underarm and shoulder seams.

Right sides together, pin facing to one armhole of dress, matching notches. Stitch right round armhole edge. Layer and clip seam, press facing to wrong side. Neaten raw edge of facing, and catch to dress at shoulder and underarm seams with a few neat stitches. Stitch other armhole facings together in a similar way, and stitch to other armhole of dress.

Turn up hem at lower edge of dress to length required, and stitch neatly.

To make belt, fold belt section in half lengthwise, right sides together. Stitch round all open edges, leaving a gap in the seam. Turn belt right side out, turn in seam allowance on open edge and slip-stitch opening closed. Stitch short straight edge over bar of buckle.

Long-sleeved dress

Make as for sleeveless dress, but omit neck facing, sleeve arm-hole facing, and belt instructions. Instead, after stitching dress front to back, fold collar section in half lengthwise, right sides together. Stitch down each short edge. Trim seam, and turn collar right side out. Press.

Right sides together, pin collar to right side of dress neck edge, matching notches. Stitch, taking stitching through dress fabric and single layer of collar only. Layer and clip seam. Turn in seam allowance on remaining open edge of collar and slip-stitch neatly by hand to inside of neck edge seam just stitched.

On each sleeve, stitch dart, as indicated by guide lines on pattern. Run two rows of gathering stitches round head of sleeves, as indicated on pattern. Right sides together, stitch underarm seam. Turn under cuff lower edge, as marked by fold line on pattern, and stitch neatly.

Sew sleeves into armholes of dress, matching notches, and adjusting gathers to fit.

Sew hook and eye to centre back neck edge, above zipper.

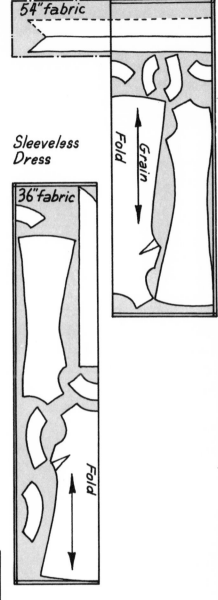

Sleeveless Dress

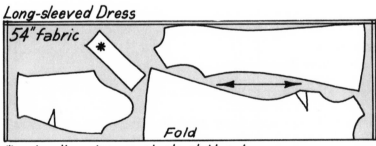

Long-sleeved Dress

Fold

Cutting-out layouts

✻ *cut collar piece on single cloth only*

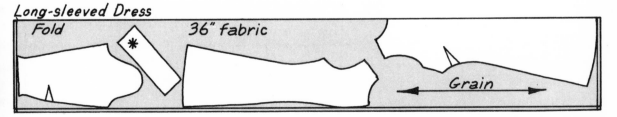

Long-sleeved Dress

155

Two-way shift dress

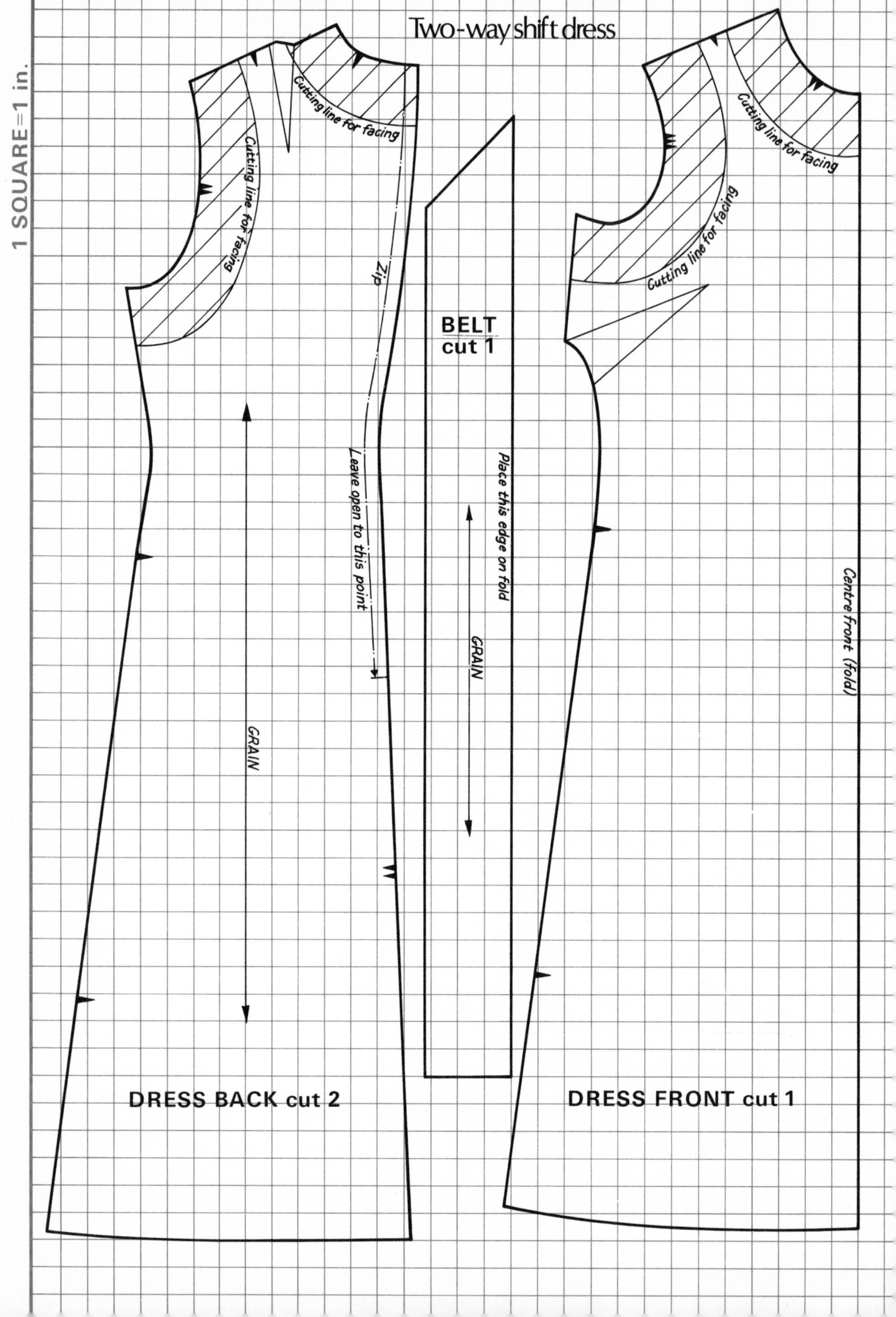

1 SQUARE = 1 in.

BELT cut 1

Cutting line for facing

Cutting line for facing

Cutting line for facing

Cutting line for facing

Zip

Leave open to this point

Place this edge on fold

GRAIN

GRAIN

Centre front (fold)

DRESS BACK cut 2

DRESS FRONT cut 1

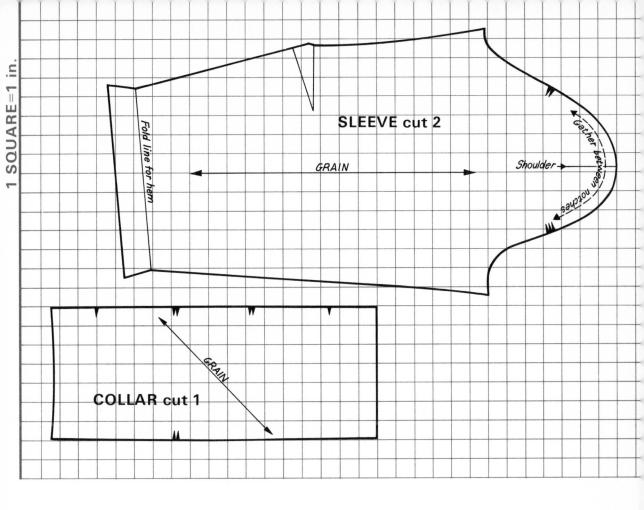

1 SQUARE=1 in.

SLEEVE cut 2

Fold line for hem

GRAIN

Shoulder →

Gather between notches

COLLAR cut 1

GRAIN

Separates - for day and evening

illustrated in colour on page 126

From this one pattern you can make a pretty, long-sleeved blouse and a skirt in two lengths—long and straight for evening, short and pleated for day.

MATERIALS

For blouse and long skirt: $3\frac{3}{4}$yd. of fabric, 48in. wide (for blouse only: $2\frac{1}{4}$yd. of fabric, 36in. wide); five $\frac{1}{2}$-in. buttons; a 9-in. zipper; 2 hooks and eyes; $\frac{5}{8}$yd. of interfacing, 32 or 36in. wide. **For short skirt:** $1\frac{7}{8}$yd. of fabric, 36in. wide, or $1\frac{1}{8}$yd. of fabric, 54in. wide; a 9-in. zipper; 1 hook and eye; a bought belt; $\frac{3}{8}$yd. of interfacing, 32 or 36in. wide.

FABRIC SUGGESTIONS

Our blouse and long skirt are made up in a printed Tricel jersey; the short skirt is made up in a Digoloom white wool, with top-stitching in black, and a bought black belt.

SIZE NOTE

The pattern as given will comfortably fit bust size 34in., hip size 36in. To adapt the pattern to fit a bigger or smaller size, see page 106.

TO MAKE YOUR PATTERN

The diagram on pages 161–2 gives the pieces you need. One square on the diagram equals 1in. Prepare your full-size pattern on squared paper, following instructions on page 106. Cut out fabric, following cutting-out layouts on page 160. Place skirt front and bodice back on fold of fabric as indicated to avoid seams at these points in the garment.

Cut 2 front facings, 1 collar section and 1 waistband section (only half width) from interfacing for long skirt and blouse; cut 2 pocket sections and 1 waistband section (only half width) from interfacing for short skirt. From fabric for short skirt, cut 4 strips, each 3 in. by $1\frac{1}{4}$in., for belt carriers.

Unless otherwise stated, all seams should be stitched $\frac{5}{8}$in. from the edge of the fabric; press all seams open after stitching.

TO MAKE
Blouse

Stitch bust darts in blouse fronts, and back shoulder darts in blouse back, as indicated by guide lines on the pattern. Right sides together, stitch fronts to back at shoulders and side seams. Iron on or baste on interfacing to wrong side of front facing sections. Fold facings to right side of blouse front as indicated by fold line on pattern. Stitch from fold at neck edge as far as centre front. Trim and clip seam allowance. Turn right side out and press well.

Iron on or baste on interfacing to wrong side of one collar section (this will be top collar). Place top collar and undercollar together, right sides facing, and stitch right round outer edges (leave neck edges unstitched). Layer and clip seam allowance, and turn collar right side out. Press well. Place collar in position on blouse, lining up neck edges, matching notches, and having undercollar facing right side of blouse. Fold facings over on to collar, lining up neck edges, so right side of facings are against top collar.

Stitch round neck seam, stitching through all fabric thickness on front of blouse as far as shoulder seams, and then through blouse fabric and undercollar only at back neck.

Layer and clip seam carefully.

Turn in seam allowance on back neck edge of top collar and slip-stitch by hand over inside of neck edge seam just stitched. Turn front facings to inside; neaten long raw edges, turn in seam allowance on short (shoulder) edges and slip-stitch by hand neatly to inside of shoulder seams of blouse. Make five hand-worked buttonholes on right front, in positions marked on pattern.

Right sides together, stitch underarm seam in each sleeve. Work two rows of gathering stitching round lower edge as marked on pattern. Right sides together, stitch short edges of each cuff together. Pin one cuff in position to lower edge of one sleeve, right sides together, lining up cuff seam with sleeve underarm seam, and adjusting gathers on sleeve to fit cuff.

Stitch round entire cuff edge. Press seam towards cuff. Fold cuff in half to wrong side, turn in seam allowance on remaining edge, and slip-stitch by hand to inside of seam just stitched. Set sleeves into armholes of blouse, matching notches and easing head of sleeves to fit armholes, as marked on pattern. Open out front facings and stitch a narrow hem round entire lower edge of blouse. Fold back facings, and slip-stitch neatly to hem along lower edge. Sew on buttons to left front, to correspond with buttonholes, and sew a hook and eye to fasten neck edge of blouse.

Long skirt

Stitch darts on front and back sections, as marked by guide lines on pattern. Right sides together, stitch centre back seam, leaving seam open from waist edge as marked for the zipper. Sew zipper into this opening. Right sides together, stitch skirt front to back at side seams.

Fold waistband section in half lengthwise, right sides together, and iron on or baste on interfacing to one side of it. Stitch down both short edges, and along long edge at one end only for $1\frac{1}{2}$in. Pin waistband to right side of skirt, having the $1\frac{1}{2}$-in. extension at right back centre opening. Stitch round waist seam, stitching through skirt fabric and one thickness of waistband fabric only. Clip seam and press up. Turn in seam allowance on remaining edge of waistband and slip-stitch by hand to inside of waist seam.

Turn up hem at lower edge to length required and stitch neatly. Sew on hook and eye to fasten waistband at centre back opening.

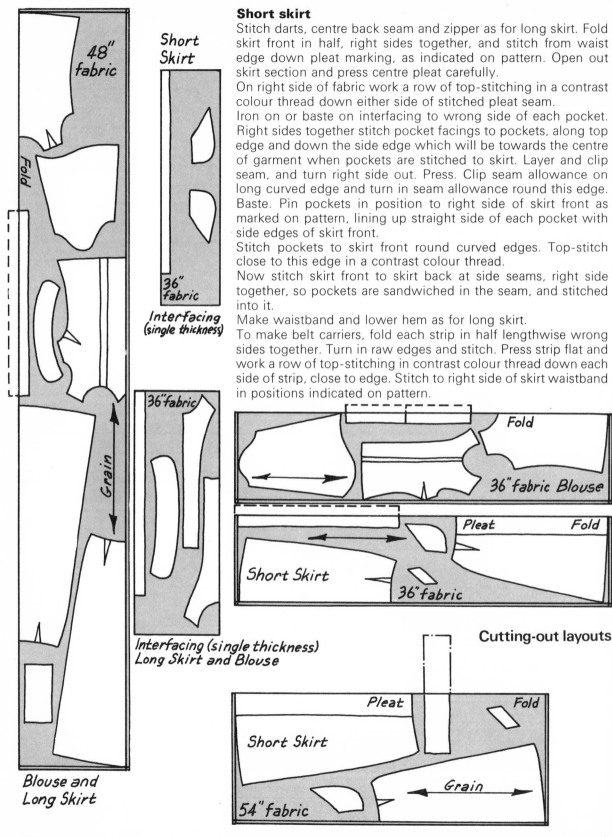

48″ fabric

Short Skirt

Fold

36″ fabric

Interfacing (single thickness)

Grain

36″ fabric

Interfacing (single thickness) Long Skirt and Blouse

Blouse and Long Skirt

Short skirt

Stitch darts, centre back seam and zipper as for long skirt. Fold skirt front in half, right sides together, and stitch from waist edge down pleat marking, as indicated on pattern. Open out skirt section and press centre pleat carefully.

On right side of fabric work a row of top-stitching in a contrast colour thread down either side of stitched pleat seam.

Iron on or baste on interfacing to wrong side of each pocket. Right sides together stitch pocket facings to pockets, along top edge and down the side edge which will be towards the centre of garment when pockets are stitched to skirt. Layer and clip seam, and turn right side out. Press. Clip seam allowance on long curved edge and turn in seam allowance round this edge. Baste. Pin pockets in position to right side of skirt front as marked on pattern, lining up straight side of each pocket with side edges of skirt front.

Stitch pockets to skirt front round curved edges. Top-stitch close to this edge in a contrast colour thread.

Now stitch skirt front to skirt back at side seams, right side together, so pockets are sandwiched in the seam, and stitched into it.

Make waistband and lower hem as for long skirt.

To make belt carriers, fold each strip in half lengthwise wrong sides together. Turn in raw edges and stitch. Press strip flat and work a row of top-stitching in contrast colour thread down each side of strip, close to edge. Stitch to right side of skirt waistband in positions indicated on pattern.

Fold

36″ fabric Blouse

Pleat *Fold*

Short Skirt

36″ fabric

Cutting-out layouts

Pleat *Fold*

Short Skirt

Grain

54″ fabric

1 SQUARE=1 in.

Separates-for day and evening

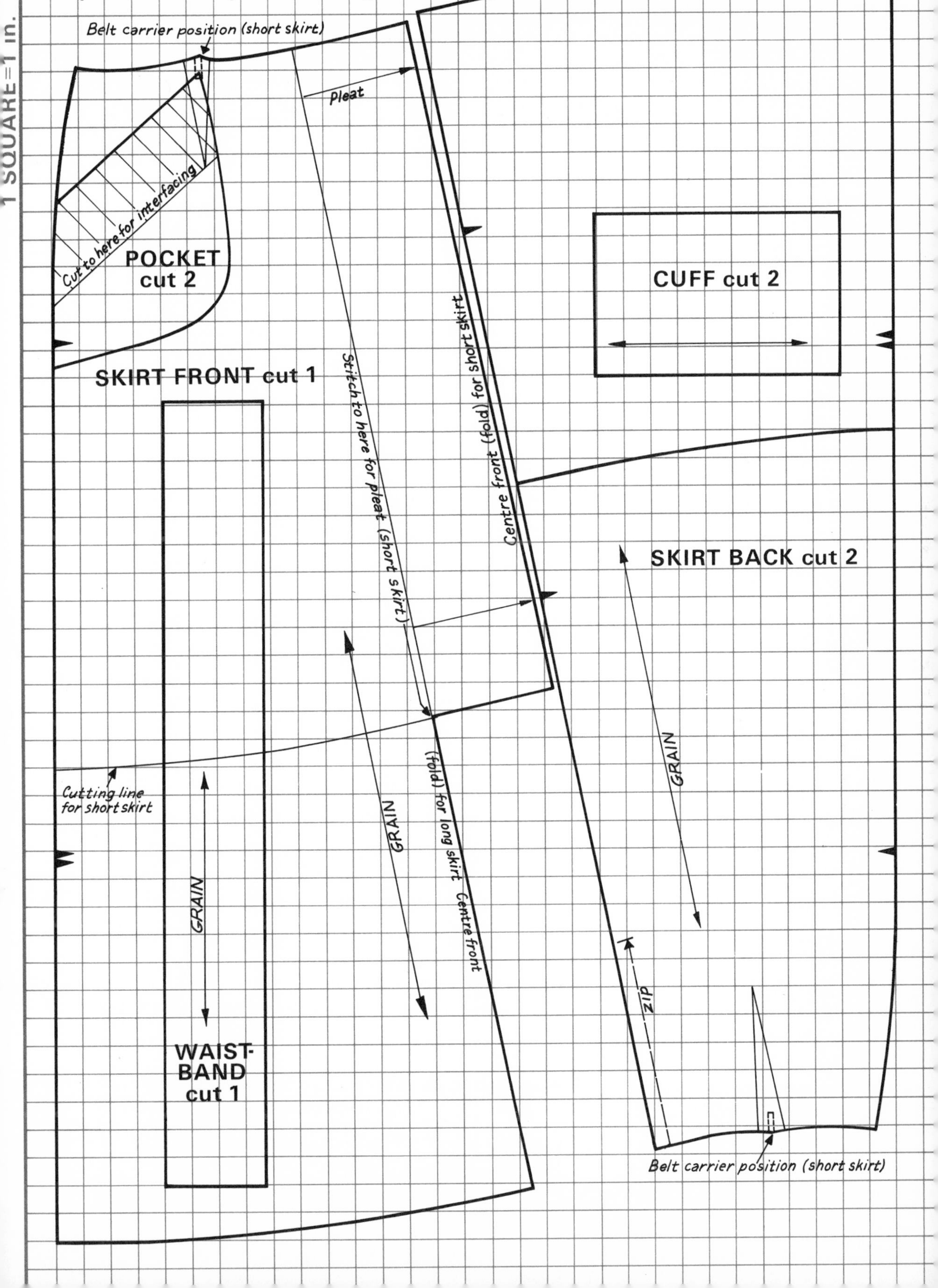

Belt carrier position (short skirt)

Pleat

Cut to here for interfacing

POCKET
cut 2

SKIRT FRONT cut 1

CUFF cut 2

Stitch to here for pleat (short skirt)

Centre front (fold) for short skirt

SKIRT BACK cut 2

GRAIN

Cutting line
for short skirt

GRAIN

(fold) for long skirt Centre front

GRAIN

ZIP

WAIST-
BAND
cut 1

Belt carrier position (short skirt)

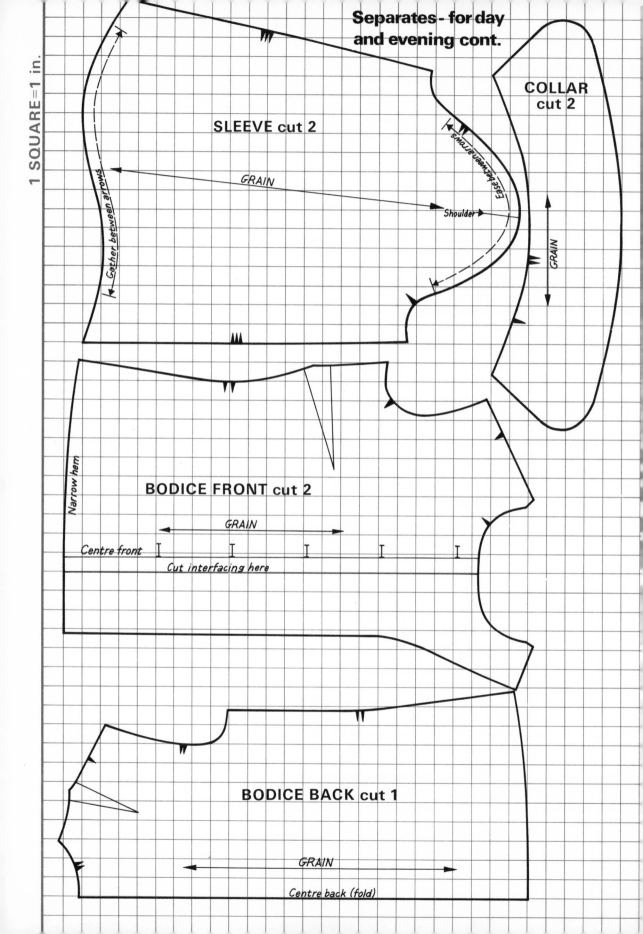

1 SQUARE = 1 in.

Separates - for day and evening cont.

SLEEVE cut 2

GRAIN

Gather between arrows

Shoulder

Ease between arrows

COLLAR
cut 2

GRAIN

BODICE FRONT cut 2

Narrow hem

GRAIN

Centre front

Cut interfacing here

BODICE BACK cut 1

GRAIN

Centre back (fold)

Classic suit and blouse-
for a larger size

illustrated in colour on page 90

MATERIALS
For suit: $2\frac{1}{2}$yd. of fabric, 60in. wide; $\frac{1}{2}$yd. of interfacing, 36in. wide; four $\frac{3}{4}$-in. buttons; a waist length of petersham ribbon, 1in. wide; 1 hook and eye; an 8-in. zipper. **For blouse:** $2\frac{1}{2}$yd. of fabric, 36in. wide; five $\frac{1}{2}$-in. buttons.

FABRIC SUGGESTIONS
Our suit is made up in a bonded Courtelle by Epatra; the blouse is made up in a printed pique cotton.

SIZE NOTE
The pattern as given will comfortably fit bust size 38in., hip size 40in. To adapt the pattern to fit a bigger or smaller size, see page 106.

TO MAKE YOUR PATTERN
The diagram on pages 165—6 gives the pieces you need. One square on the diagram equals 1in. Prepare your full-size pattern on squared paper, following instructions on page 106. Cut out fabric, following cutting-out layouts on page 164. Place skirt front, jacket back neck facing and blouse back on fold of fabric, as indicated, to avoid seams at these points in the garment. Cut 2 front facings, and 1 back neck facing from interfacing. Unless otherwise stated, all seams should be stitched $\frac{5}{8}$in. from the edge of fabric; press all seams open after stitching.

TO MAKE
Jacket
Stitch bust darts and back shoulder darts in jacket fronts and backs, as marked by guide lines on pattern pieces. Right sides together, stitch centre back seam.
Join front to back, right sides facing, at shoulder and side seams. Iron on or baste on interfacing to wrong sides of front and back neck facing sections. Right sides together, stitch facings at shoulder seams. Right sides together, pin facings in position to jacket. Stitch right round front and back neck edges. Layer and clip seam. Turn facings to inside of jacket. Neaten raw edges of facing, and catch facing to shoulder seams of jacket with a few neat stitches. Make hand-worked buttonholes on right front of jacket in positions marked.
Right sides together, stitch each undersleeve to each top sleeve, matching notches.
Turn under lower edge of each sleeve on fold line marked, and hem-stitch neatly in position. Set sleeves into armholes of jacket, matching notches, and easing sleeves to fit armholes between arrows marked.
Open out lower front facings, and turn up and stitch hem round

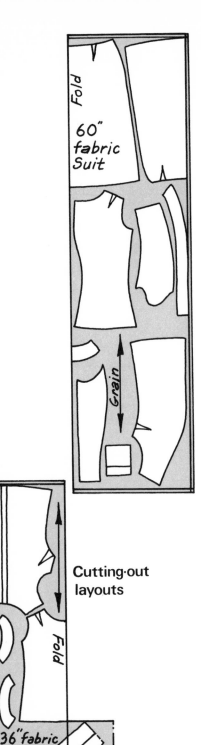

lower edge of jacket. Fold back facings, and slip-stitch to hem at lower edge.

Make patch pockets, following instructions on page 42, and stitch to jacket in positions marked on pattern.

Work saddle stitching—large running stitches worked $\frac{1}{2}$in. from edge of garment—in a contrasting thread colour round entire front edges, along tops of pockets, and lower edges of sleeves. Sew on buttons to left front to correspond with buttonholes.

Skirt

Stitch waist darts in skirt front and back sections, as marked by guide lines on pattern. Right sides together, stitch centre back seam. Right sides together, stitch skirt front to backs at side seams, leaving left side open from waist down as marked on pattern. Stitch zipper into this opening.

Pin petersham ribbon to right side of waist edge, and stitch. Press petersham to wrong side. Turn up lower hem to length required and stitch neatly. Sew hook and eye to fasten waist edge above zipper.

Blouse

Stitch bust darts and back shoulder darts in front and back sections, as marked by guide lines on pattern. Right sides together stitch front to back, at shoulder and side seams. Fold front facings on to right side along fold line marked. Stitch along neck edge from fold as far as notch marking for tie. Trim and clip seam, and turn facing to wrong side. Press well. Make worked buttonholes on blouse right front in positions marked on pattern.

Right sides together, stitch collar and tie sections together at centre back seam. Fold entire strip in half lengthwise, right sides together. Stitch down each short edge and along long edge as far as notch marking for tie. Trim and clip seam, and turn tie right side out. Press well.

Pin collar in place to right side of neck edge of blouse. Stitch in place stitching only through blouse fabric and single thickness of collar. Layer and clip seam and turn in seam allowance on remaining edge of collar. Slip-stitch neatly by hand to wrong side of neck seam just stitched.

Right sides together, stitch each pair of armhole facings together at shoulder and underarm seams.

Pin facings to armholes of blouse, right sides facing, and matching underarm and shoulder seams. Stitch. Layer and clip seams. Neaten outer edge of facings. Turn to wrong side and catch to underarm and shoulder seams of blouse with a few neat stitches. Open out front facings, and turn up and stitch narrow hem round lower edge of blouse. Fold back facings and slip-stitch to hem at lower edge. Sew on buttons to correspond with buttonholes.

Cutting-out layouts

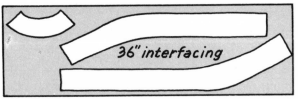

1 SQUARE = 1 in.

Classic suit and blouse

FRONT cut 2

Cutting line for facing and interfacing

Saddle stitching

POCKET cut 2

GRAIN

fold line

Saddle stitching

TOP SLEEVE cut 2

Ease between arrows

shoulder

Saddle stitching

fold line for hem

BACK cut 2

Saddle stitching

Cutting line for facing & interfacing

GRAIN

Centre back

BLOUSE BACK cut 1

Cutting line facing

GRAIN

Centre back (fold)

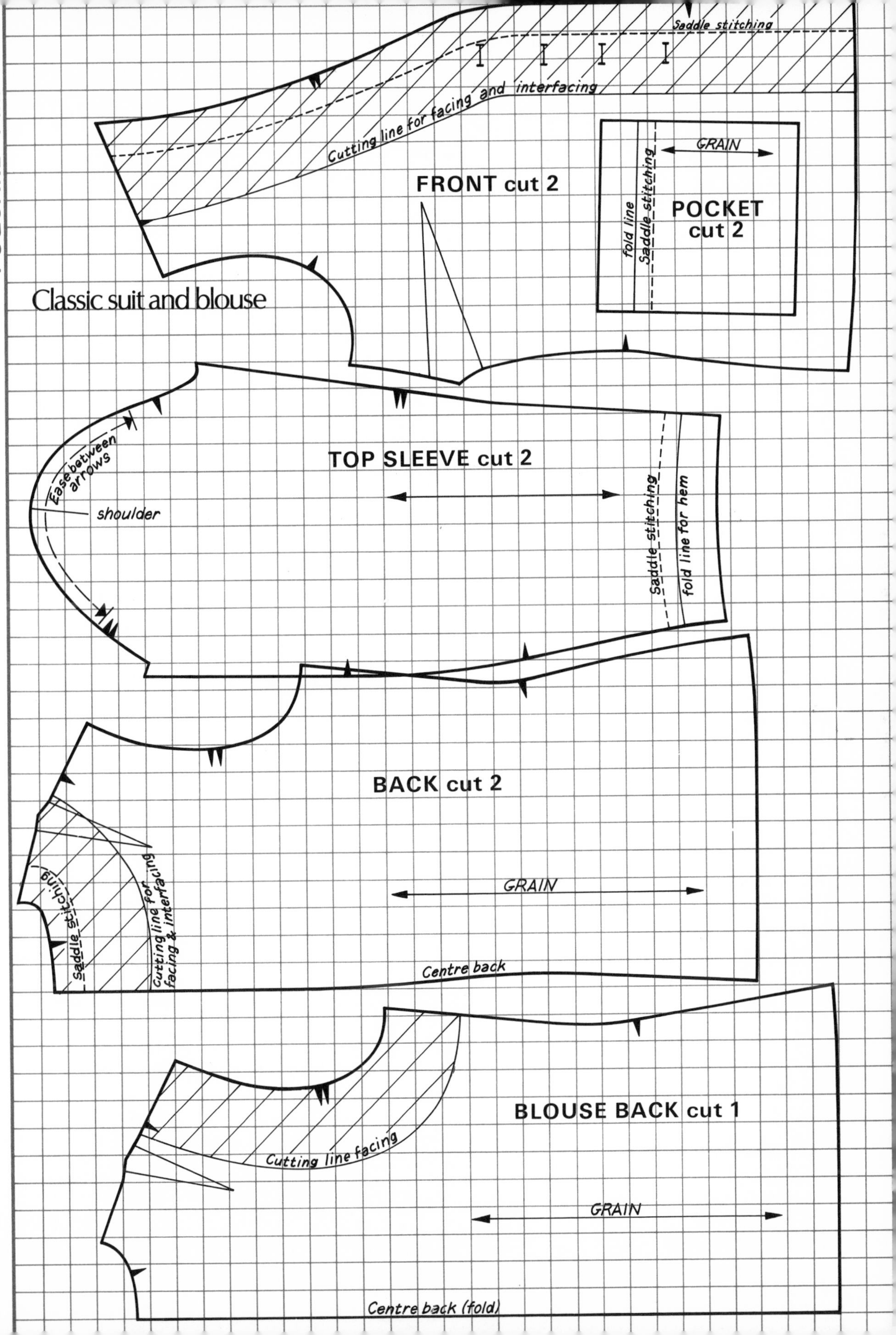

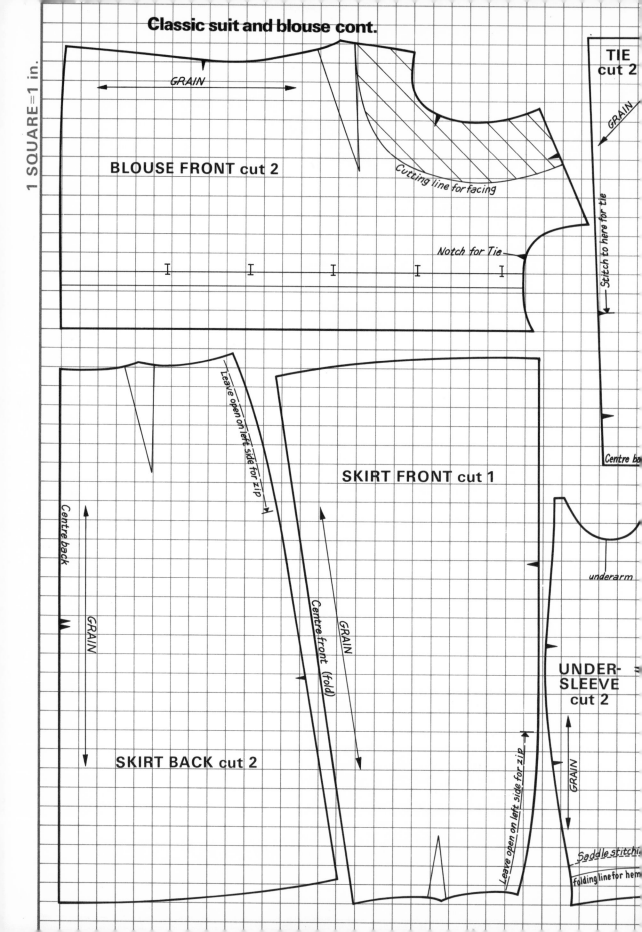

1 SQUARE=1 in.

TIE
cut 2

GRAIN

GRAIN

BLOUSE FRONT cut 2

Cutting line for facing

Stitch to here for tie

Notch for Tie

Centre ba

Leave open on left side for zip

SKIRT FRONT cut 1

Centre back

Centre front (fold)

GRAIN

GRAIN

underarm

UNDER-
SLEEVE
cut 2

GRAIN

GRAIN

SKIRT BACK cut 2

Leave open on left side for zip

Saddle stitchi

folding line for hem

Cape

illustrated in colour on page 107

MATERIALS
$2\frac{3}{4}$yd. of fabric, 54in. wide; $4\frac{1}{4}$yd. of lining fabric, 36in. wide; $1\frac{1}{4}$yd. of interfacing, 32 or 36in. wide; five 1-in. buttons.

FABRIC SUGGESTION
Our cape is made up in a wool tweed by Digoloom.

SIZE NOTE
The pattern as given will comfortably fit bust size 34/36in., hip size 36/38in. To adapt the pattern to fit a bigger or smaller size, see page 106.

TO MAKE YOUR PATTERN
The diagram on pages 169–70 gives the pieces you need. One square on the diagram equals 1in. Prepare your full-size pattern on squared paper, following instructions on page 106. Cut out fabric, following cutting-out layouts on page 168. Place cape back on fold of fabric, as indicated (follow centre back marking on pattern piece). Cut cape front, side front and back from lining fabric, using full width of back pattern piece. Cut front facing and collar from interfacing.
Unless otherwise stated, all seams should be stitched $\frac{5}{8}$in. from the edge of fabric; press all seams open after stitching.

TO MAKE
Stitch back neck darts in cape back as indicated by guide lines on pattern.
Right sides together, stitch cape fronts to side fronts, matching notches and leaving seam open as marked on pattern pieces. Turn in seam allowance on the openings and baste. Press well.
Right sides together, stitch cape fronts to back at side seams. Baste on or iron on interfacing to wrong side of cape fronts, as marked on pattern.
Iron on or baste on interfacing to wrong side of one collar section (this will be the top collar). Place collar sections right sides together, and stitch together round all edges, except neck edges.
Place collar in position to right side of cape neck edge, matching notches, having top collar facing cape. Keep front facings opened out so they do not get in the way. Stitch neck seam, stitching through all thicknesses of fabric. Clip seam and press down. Turn collar up.
Fold front facings to wrong side, turn in seam allowance on neck edges, and slip-stitch neatly by hand to inside of neck seam just stitched.
Make five hand-worked buttonholes in right front of cape at positions marked on pattern.

Open out facings, and turn up hem to length required. Stitch. Fold back facings and slip-stitch to hem along lower edge. Make up lining: right sides together stitch centre back seam. Pleat as indicated on pattern and baste to hold in place. Right sides together, stitch lining front to side front, leaving seam open as marked, then stitch back to fronts at side seams. Turn up and stitch lower hem in lining.

Place lining in position to cape, wrong sides together. Turn in raw edges round front and neck edges, and round arm slit openings, and slip-stitch neatly to cape.

Sew on buttons to left front to correspond with buttonholes.

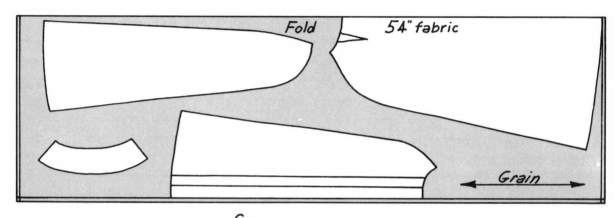

Cape

Cutting-out layouts

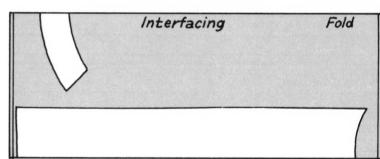

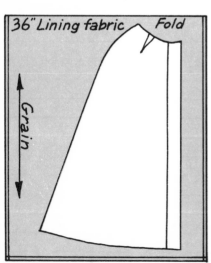

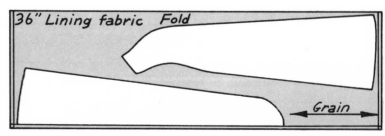

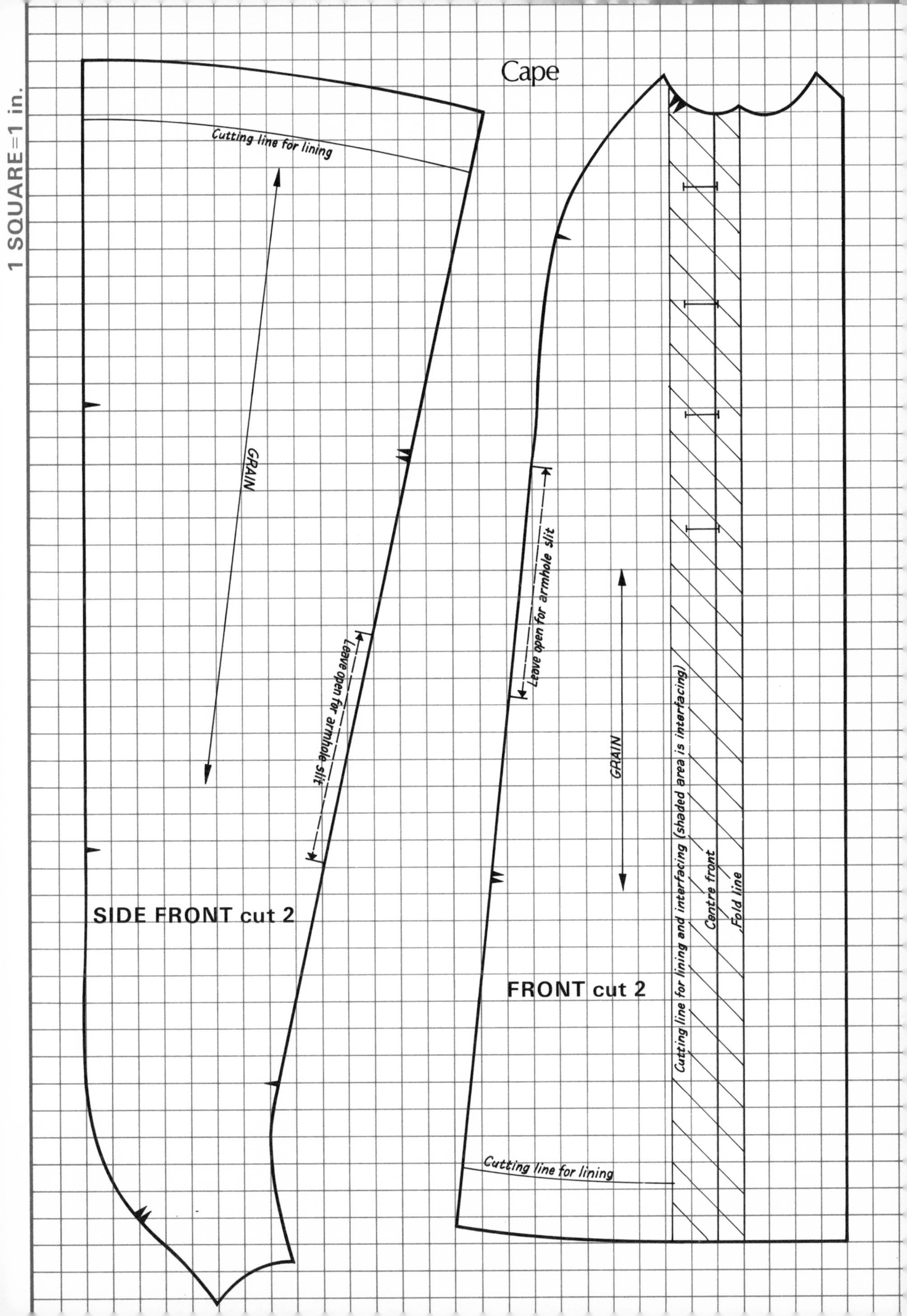

1 SQUARE=1 in.

Cape

Cutting line for lining

GRAIN

Cutting line for lining

Leave open for armhole slit

Leave open for armhole slit

GRAIN

Cutting line for lining and interfacing (shaded area is interfacing)

Centre front

Fold line

SIDE FRONT cut 2

FRONT cut 2

Cutting line for lining

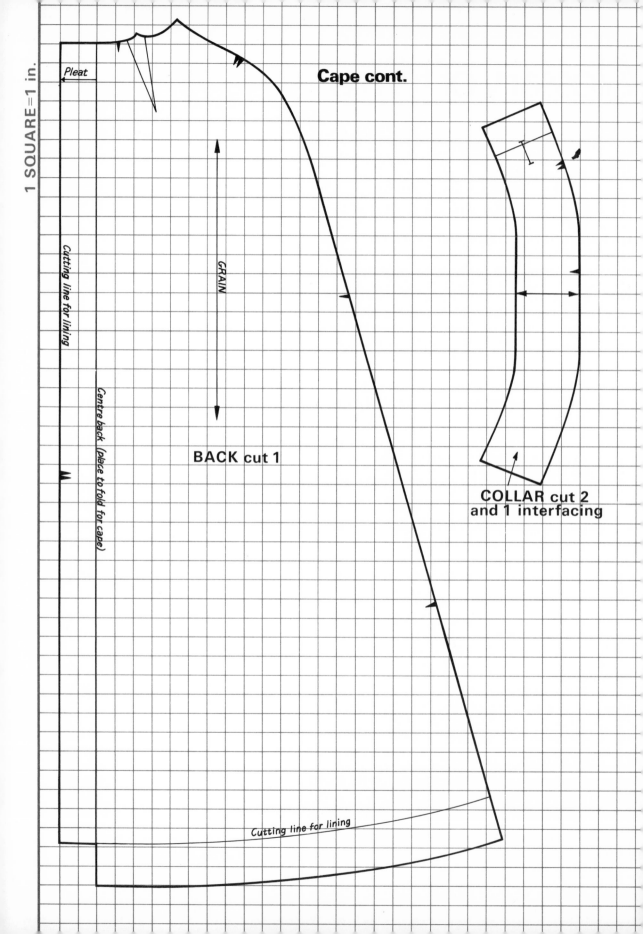

1 SQUARE=1 in.

Pleat

Cutting line for lining

Centre back (place to fold for cape)

GRAIN

Cape cont.

BACK cut 1

Cutting line for lining

COLLAR cut 2 and 1 interfacing

Glossary of terms

Alteration lines. Double lines given on certain pattern pieces indicating where the pattern should be adjusted to lengthen or shorten before cutting.

Armhole. Opening in a garment for the arm; line on which a set-in sleeve is sewn to the garment.

Arrow. On seam line: indicates direction for cutting and stitching with the grain of the fabric. On a pattern piece: heavy double-pointed arrows indicate straight grain of fabric.

Back-stitching. Stitching to secure the thread ends at the beginning and end of a stitching line. Place needle in fabric about $\frac{1}{4}$in. in from the start of the stitching line and stitch backward to the starting point; then stitch forward. At end of the stitching line, stitch backward $\frac{1}{4}$in.

Basting. Temporary stitching or pinning to hold two or more pieces of fabric together until they are permanently stitched. Hand-basting: sew by hand with long stitches. Machine-basting: sew by machine using the longest stitch. Do not fasten ends or work back-stitching. Before removing stitches, snip threads every few inches. Pin-basting: hold together by using pins. Use enough pins to keep two layers of fabric from slipping. Place pins so they can be easily removed as you stitch the seam.

Bias. Any diagonal direction away from the straight lengthwise or crosswise grain of a fabric. The true bias is the diagonal line formed when a fabric is folded so crosswise threads run in the same direction as lengthwise threads.

Bias binding or tape. Single or double fold of strips cut on true bias and stitched to garment edges as a finish or trim.

Clip. To cut into the seam allowance almost to the stitching-line. Used on curved seams where one edge must spread to fit another section of the garment; also used on curved seams that must lie flat when turned.

Dart. A stitched fold, tapering to a point at one end, or from the centre to points at both ends; used to fit a garment.

Directional stitching. Stitching in the direction that is with the grain of the fabric.

Ease. Slight extra length in one seam edge not found in the edge to which it is joined. Usually marked on the pattern with the word 'ease'. Also, tolerance or the extra room designed into certain parts of a pattern for comfort and easy movement in the finished garment.

Edge stitching. Line of stitching done close to any folded edge or seamline, about $\frac{1}{8}$in. from the edge.

Face. To finish an edge by applying a fitted piece of the same or another fabric.

Gather. To draw up fabric on a line of stitching.

Grain. Lengthwise and crosswise threads of a fabric.

Interfacing. Material for shaping, reinforcing, stiffening or giving body to certain sections of a garment.

Interlining. Fabric cut in the same shape of the outer fabric and used in coats and jackets for warmth. Constructed separately and placed between lining and outer fabric.

Layer. To trim seam allowances to different widths to reduce the bulk and give a flatter, smoother look. Generally used in inside seams.

Mitre. To form a diagonal seam at a square corner of a hem or a straight band.

Overcasting. Hand-stitching on raw edges to prevent fabric from fraying. The stitch is done from either direction with slanting stitches from $\frac{1}{8}$in. to $\frac{1}{4}$in. in depth.

Pink. To finish an edge by cutting with pinking shears.

Pivot. To turn a square corner by leaving the needle in the fabric, lifting the presser foot and turning the material being stitched in another direction.

Pleat. Fold of fabric, usually not stitched down, but may be partially stitched; used for fitting, for comfort or decoration.

Seam allowance. The distance from the edge of the cut fabric to the point where stitching is worked. In most patterns the seam allowance usually is $\frac{5}{8}$in.

Selvedge. The narrow, firmly-woven finished edge along both lengthwise edges of a fabric.

Slip-stitch. An invisible hand-sewing for finishing hems or facings, or for joining edges of an opening. On hems or facings, take up one thread in the under fabric and slip needle in fold of one edge.

Stay-stitching. A line of regular stitching done on bias or curved edges that are to be joined to another piece to hold the grain so it does not stretch in handling.

Tailor's tacks. Temporary basting stitches made through two thicknesses of fabric and then cut apart. Used to mark construction symbols.

Top-stitching. Stitching made on the outside of the garment. It may be close to a seamline, or for a decorative effect $\frac{1}{4}$in. or more from an edge.

Underlining. Shaping material that is attached to the garment piece before any other stitching is done so all construction is done on both layers of fabric and treated as a single thickness.

Understitching. Used to describe top-stitching done on the inside very close to a seamline so the stitching and seam will not show. Used on facings.

Acknowledgements

Acknowledgements are due to the following people and organisations who generously gave help with the preparation of this book:

Bondina Vilene Ltd.
Digoloom Fabrics Ltd.
English Sewing Ltd.
Epatra Fabrics Ltd.
Mrs. Stella Dick—who designed all the clothes in the pattern chapter.
The Singer Company (UK) Ltd.—photographs on pages 17, 20 and 21 show Singer sewing machines, photographs on pages 17, 18 and 83 show examples of stitching worked on Singer machines.
Simplicity Patterns Ltd.—photographs on pages 8, 23, 35, 36, 38, 40, 53, 56, 65, 77, 80, 86, 88, 92, 94, 97, 98, 100, 102 and 105 all show clothes from the Simplicity range of paper patterns. Similar designs should be found in the current Simplicity pattern catalogue.
Sew-Rite Fabrics, 120 The Centre, Feltham, Middlesex—who loaned the sewing materials and accessories shown in the jacket photograph.

Index